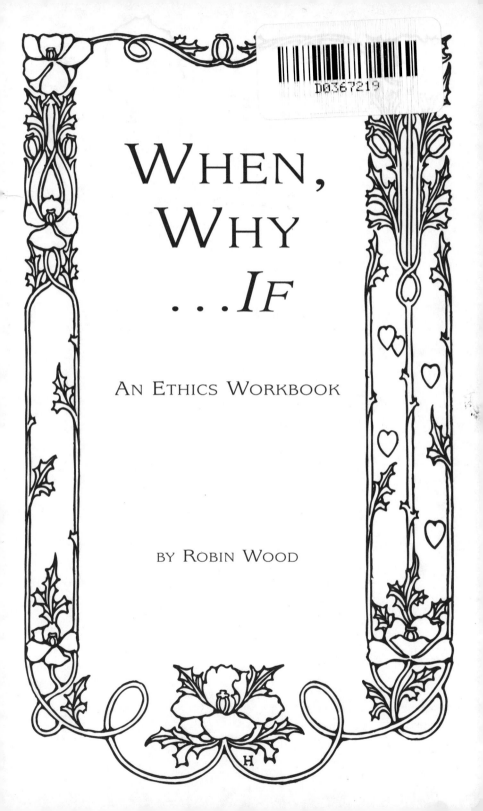

WHEN, WHY ...IF

AN ETHICS WORKBOOK

BY ROBIN WOOD

WHEN, WHY ...IF

A Livingtree Book / December 1996

All rights reserved

Copyright © 1996 by Robin Wood

Library of Congress Catalog Card Number: 96-094636

ISBN: 0-9652984-0-X

Book Design by Robin Wood

Cover © Robin Wood 1996

Decorations by Theodore B. Hapgood 1906

Fonts: Usherwood Book, Bold & Italic; Nadianne

For information contact:
Robin Wood
3319 Greenfield Suite 102
Dearborn, MI 48120

TABLE OF CONTENTS

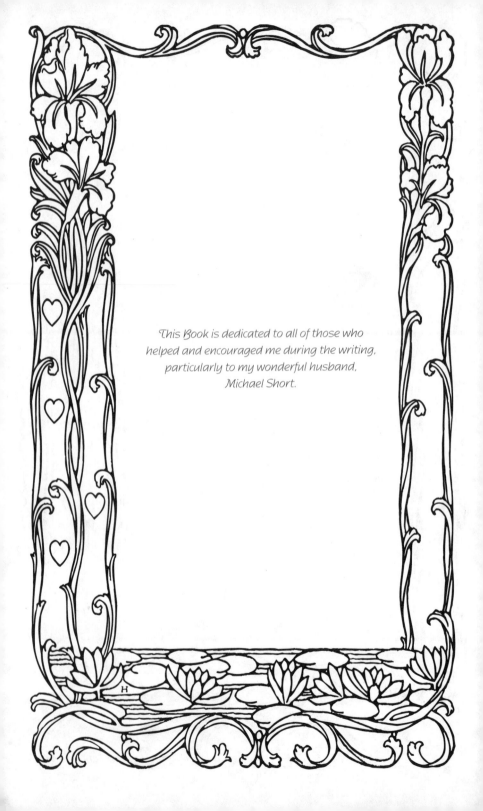

This Book is dedicated to all of those who helped and encouraged me during the writing, particularly to my wonderful husband, Michael Short.

INTRODUCTION

Book; Reader. Reader; Book.

I know introductions are often boring, but please read this one.

In this book, we shall explore the moral and ethical basis for Wicca, Paganism, and the New Age.

Long ago, when the Old Religion was the Only Religion, all of this was taught during infancy and childhood, and everyone understood their ethical obligations to the world around them.

With the rise of the Patriarchal Religions, ethics and morals were gradually replaced by an increasingly complex code of behavior. Laws and rules to govern every aspect of life were written down and every letter of the law was strictly adhered to. Lists of "do" and "do not" appeared until people lost all sense of the reasoning behind the laws, and obedience became the highest virtue. At last, the law became everything, to be followed blindly; and most people conformed either to the camp of "anything not strictly forbidden is allowed" or "anything not specifically allowed is forbidden" depending on their own temperament and that of their society.

Anyone who erred in following the code either asked for forgiveness from God, which he granted instantly and completely through his divine mercy; or asked for forgiveness from God, performed the penance his priests required of them, and then were granted forgiveness instantly and completely, see above.

In either case it was God that had to be appealed to, because it was His Law that had been broken.

There are no gray areas here, no moral dilemmas, just right and wrong simple and clear cut. There are no natural consequences for your actions, no personal responsibility for any outcome, no reasoning, no thinking of any kind required; in short no ethics at all, just a list of things to be memorized, and a simple formula of repentance and forgiveness if you forget or decide to skip one.

How simple. How easy.

You can see why it caught on.

It's how most of us were raised.

But there is something about it that you don't like, or you would not be reading this book.

Don't think for a moment, though, that ours is the easier path. On this road, you are required to have your brain with you at all times.

Here we have no written laws to follow, no codes, no repentance and forgiveness. Unless this is the first book about the Craft that you have ever read, chances are that you have already encountered the "do as you will" bit, and may have grown rather heady with the freedom of it. Most of us do.

This was fine, as long as everyone who was seeking had a teacher; an actual flesh-and-blood to have conversations and long discussions with. Someone who was an experienced counselor and practitioner of our Art. Then ethical codes could be discussed, problems could be presented for solving, practice cases could come up, and all of this stuff could be explored and guidance given right along with everything else that makes up our Craft.

But more and more students are learning from books alone, unable to find a teacher or even to find out how to find one. And many of the books available seem to concentrate on the "how to" instead of on the "why would you?" or even "should you?" behind the Craft.

As I travel around the country, selling prints and tarot decks at science fiction conventions, I increasingly find that folk are coming to me with questions. Folk who have initiated themselves, and then initiated their friends, into a system based partially on a book or two about the Craft, and partially on science-fiction or fantasy novels and movies – and then moving on with no moral sense

beyond a vague, fuzzy "harm none" or "let the Force be with you."

Dear friend, this is not enough to base your actions on.

Everything that you do, or don't do, has consequences that ripple through the world like a pebble dropped into a pond, and you are responsible for them!

There is no instant repentance and forgiveness. The three-fold law is a law like gravity, not a statute. Everything you do, either for good or ill, will come back to you three times. And if you choose to ignore this, or are ignorant of it, or just plain make a mistake, and harm someone the only way to avoid getting three times as much harm back is to run right out and fix it! You have to help them three times as much as you harmed them, as quickly as possible.

Far from acting with complete moral license, an experienced Witch should be one of the most moral creatures on the planet.

And yet, from the questions I am asked and the stories I am told, I fear that this is not so.

So, for all of you who are earnestly seeking and have no one to teach you, for all who long to be the best you that you can possibly become, for all who are seeking to win through to the light, and all who are trying to find the balance point, I offer this book, with all my love.

Listen, and learn to find the wisdom hidden within.

And because I hate dry, boring, pedantic books, and because I love laughter, and because all acts of Joy are Holy to Her, I will try to make it as interesting and funny as I can.

Even though I am altogether too fond of run-on sentences and bad jokes!

CHAPTER 1 - THE BEGINNING

*The White Rabbit put on his spectacles.
"Where shall I begin, please your Majesty?"
he asked.*

*"Begin at the beginning," the King said,
gravely, "and go on till you come to the end:
then stop."*

– Lewis Carroll, Alice in Wonderland

As I sat down to start writing this book, I
found that the hardest part was to decide
where to begin.

Ordinarily, this is not a problem. When I
am working with a student, I wait until she*
begins to ask questions, and then I ask my

---

*As you have probably noticed before this, there is no
personal pronoun in English that means both male and
female. I find "s/he" to be awkward in both reading and
spelling, so I didn't want to use that. I thought about using
"she" in all cases, and telling you that verbally the female
embraces the male, and drop the "s" if you want to. Then I
thought that maybe I would just alternate "he" and "she"
whenever the need to use a pronoun arose, and explain that
this meant simply that the material was applicable to either
sex, and not that I normally teach only hermaphrodites. But
that seemed a bit weird as well, not to mention ungrammat-
ical. So I finally settled on using either "she" or "he" as the
mood struck me, but not switching sex in mid-sentence.
Everything in here, of course, is true no matter what your
sex, or your sexual preference for that matter! When you
are reading this to yourself, feel free to substitute any pronoun you may prefer.

own until she understands. Ethical problems are addressed gradually, as they come up, over the course of the year or more that it takes until the seeker is ready for initiation.*

With you that is not possible. Instead, I am having to sit down and give you all the answers at once, without any questions or even feedback from you. I am quite nervous about this process. It is not the way I like to teach; and if the need were not so great I would not even attempt it. But the need is great, so here we go. With your co-operation, we will make this work.

Ethics are an interlocking framework. It is impossible to truly understand one part without having at least some understanding of all the other parts. All through this book, I am going to be referring to things I have already told you, and things I am going to tell you, but haven't had a chance to yet, because that is how ethics work. An ethical structure is not a line, with a beginning and an end, but a sphere, with all parts resting on all the other parts.

So, I am going to go over the several parts that make up the skeleton of the ethics I am going to teach you in nine chapters (including this one.)

I am beginning with honesty, because I feel that the other parts will do you little good if

---

*See the Glossary.

you are not being honest with yourself about your actions.

At the end of each chapter, I will have ten exercises for you to do – ten of the questions I would ask you to help you put flesh on the skeleton.

I do not expect your finished system to be exactly like mine. (After all, you probably don't look a bit like me, although our skeletons have pretty much the same form and number of bones.) My answers are not necessarily your answers. That's why we have ethics in the first place, and not just a code of laws. (Of course, you already know that, because you read the Introduction. You *did* read the Introduction, didn't you?)

I also do not expect your framework of ethics to be suddenly sound, and all of your actions to be the correct ones according to that framework. I, myself, am far from perfect. I constantly make mistakes. During the writing of this book, in fact, I sometimes made mistakes that seemed so bad I thought I probably should not even be writing it.

But I do my best to learn from my mistakes, and to forgive myself, try to repair the damage, and go on.

And I have been thinking about this subject for years now. I suspect that you, too, have been thinking about it, or you wouldn't be reading this. So you can add my thinking to yours, and perhaps it will help.

I recommend that you read the entire book first, skipping the exercises. After you have finished it, go back and re-read it, starting with the chapter that you are most interested in, and wandering around if you like, doing the exercises as you go.

Whether you actually do this or not, of course, like everything else in your life is entirely up to you. And that is the root of our ethical system.

Personal responsibility.

CHAPTER 2 ~ HONESTY

*...to thine own self be true, and it shall
follow, as the night the day, thou cans't not
then be false to any man.*
~ Shakespeare, Hamlet, Act I, Scene III

Honesty, they say, is the best policy.

I, of course, heartily agree. But then I am a
Sagittarius, with Sagittarius rising and every
single planet in my natal chart above the horizon. This, according to my friend the
astrologer, is why I was 30 before I learned not
to volunteer every scrap of information I knew
to total strangers on the street whether they
wanted to hear it or not. But not everyone is
so afflicted.

Honesty, however, really is the best policy.
But what is honesty?

I lived in New Jersey for a while, and I
really, really liked it. (No, not Newark. The
Princeton area. It's quite pretty there.) In New
Jersey people tend to be brutally honest.
Anywhere else I have ever lived, when I tried
on a dress that looked horrid on me the sales-
girl would either lie outright, ("That looks really
good. You should buy it.") or be tactfully hon-

est ("That isn't very flattering. Let's see if we can find you something else.") In New Jersey, I was told "Oh no! Don't get that one! It makes you look like a couch!" I liked it. I always knew exactly where I stood, because everyone would tell me.

In most situations, tactful honesty will serve you better. After all, it gets the same result (not buying the unsuitable dress) without alienating quite so many people. Not everyone is from New Jersey.

In this chapter, though, we are going to be discussing a different sort of honesty altogether.

This is about honesty with yourself.

With yourself, you must be completely, objectively, and perfectly honest. Honestly honest, as it were.

Don't be brutal with yourself; if you were raised in this society you have probably been brutalized enough.

You will learn more, and have more to work with, if you explore the situation with your honesty. A sort of "Hmm. No, this dress doesn't look good. The print is way too large, and the chintz makes it look like an upholstery pattern. Besides that, this dirndl skirt hangs funny on me. I better go look for something more tailored, with a small print or none at all."

Do you understand the difference?

It is the difference between punishing yourself, (This dress would look fine if I was thin. I am too fat. Only hideous nasty slobs get

too fat. I think I'll go jump off a cliff,) blaming your problems on someone else, (This dress would look fine if I was thin. But I'm not, because that is the genetic hand I was dealt. Dress designers should take heavy people into account when they put these things together. It's only available in my size to make people who aren't anorexic feel bad anyway. I think I'll be nasty to the people in this store for even carrying it.) and looking at things clearly, without value judgements. (This dress would look fine if I was thin. I'll either have to lose a lot of weight, which will take a sizable investment of time and effort, or choose another dress.)

Since few of us were raised to be completely objective, this can be very hard. As small children, we were told that we were good if we pleased our parents, and bad if we did not. But they were raising us to fit in, and be obedient, so that our lives in this society would proceed smoothly. They expected us to follow the rules for our whole lives, so the "good" and "bad" judgements were necessary.

We, however, have stepped out of their framework.

In order to construct our own, we must learn to look at things honestly and fearlessly, and in order to do that, we must not pre-judge them. We have to be objective, and learn to see clearly.

We must not punish ourselves for our shortcomings. Punishment is a system

designed to help very smalls learn that certain actions have undesirable consequences. You, dear friend, are not a very small. And if you understand that the course you once chose needs changing, what possible service could punishment provide? If you want to "pay for your wrongs" isn't it more sensible to fix the undesirable outcome than to bash yourself endlessly and just let the outcome stand? And if there was no undesirable outcome, then what is the problem here?

We must not blame our problems on others. No one can "make" us do anything. Everything we do, we choose to do. In our example, being fat is generally a factor of our genetic makeup. But we are the ones who choose to read this book instead of exercising, who choose not to live on lettuce and rice cakes, who choose, indeed, to buy or not buy the societal prejudice against fat people. Ultimately, it is our choice to put a great deal of time, effort, and money into being thin; or go ahead and be fat. The fact that someone with a different genetic pattern could be thin effortlessly has no bearing on the situation. In just such a way, we can choose to rise above our physical handicaps, or we can let them dominate our lives. We can blame our parents for our bitter attitudes and our fears and distrust, or we can acknowledge that we have them and work to change them. (It's never too late to have a happy childhood.)

What we must do is look at ourselves, and our interaction with the world around us, without placing blame at all. What is past, is past. Look back and learn from it; but don't wallow in it. The future is ahead, and pliable. If you don't like the patterns you have fallen into, change them. If you don't like the future you see ahead of you, change it. (That's what this book is all about, after all!) If you don't like the way your friends and colleagues treat you, you have your choice of changing yourself until they treat you the way you wish to be treated or getting new friends and colleagues.

Once you learn to look honestly at yourself, you can change anything about yourself. Once you learn to look honestly at cause and effect, you will be able to accurately judge the effort this change will require, and decide if it is worth it. Once you learn to look honestly at the situation around you, it becomes malleable to your will. At the very least, you can change your attitude about it once you understand it.

Understanding comes with this kind of honesty.

Understanding does not mean or imply agreement or sympathy.

I can *understand* that a man beats his children because he was beaten as a child and that is all he knows, without agreeing that he should.

If I find out that a man I know is engaged in such behavior, and it is not generally

known, then I have the ethical choice of doing
nothing and allowing the children to be
beaten; calling the authorities and having the
children removed; befriending the man and
trying to persuade him to get counselling for
his own problems; befriending his wife, and
advising her to get help; befriending the children and showing them another way to solve
things so they don't pass this pattern on to
their children; and so on.

What I would actually do depends on the
age of the children, the severity of the beat-
ings, the temperament of the father (is he out
of control when he beats them, and sorry later,
or does he enjoy it?), my current relationship
with the family, and a host of other things.
There are no cut and dried answers here.
There is no fixed right and wrong. There are
only choices and outcomes, and whether I am
likely to be glad I made a particular choice, or
regret it later depends to a large extent on how
honest I am with myself about the situation.

If I know that the children's lives are in
danger, but their mother is my friend and she
begs me to do nothing, so I choose to pretend
to myself that it is not as bad as all that, what
has my dishonesty with myself caused if one
of the kids is seriously hurt, or even killed?

If I know that the children's lives are not in
danger, and their mother suggests that I mind
my own business, but I pretend to myself that
they are because I can't stand to see them hit,

what has my dishonesty caused when the authorities intervene, and the family is disrupted? If the court does nothing, because they do not consider this abusive behavior? If the court-appointed counselor engages in emotional abuse and actually damages both children and parents even more? If my former friend can no longer trust people because of my betrayal?

Do you begin to see how important the basic honesty is?

Honesty.

Clarity of vision.

Willingness to face the truth.

Willingness to act on that truth once it is faced.

Honesty.

The knowledge that we can never have all of the truth.

The willingness to admit our own mistakes.

The willingness to learn from them.

The willingness to change our minds if a new fact arises.

The willingness to forgive ourselves.

The willingness to be non-judgmental.

Honesty.

And that is only when you are learning. Now go back and reread the sentences above substituting "ability" for "willingness," and you will begin to get the hang of what we are striving for here.

Most of the ethical choices you will make, of course, will not be life-and-death, thank the Gods. Most are tiny little choices, with equally tiny little outcomes. You may think that thinking about such tiny choices is a waste of time, and you should just do whatever you feel like doing at the moment. But think of it this way, dear friend. Those little choices are practice choices; the training wheels of life. Nothing disastrous will happen, no matter which choice you make. In the grand scheme of things, it won't really matter whether you buy the chintz dress that makes you look awful, or pick another that looks good on you. It might not even occur to you that ethics have anything to do with dresses! But you can use all those tiny choices to get used to the process of making choices; of thinking clearly, honestly and objectively; of having your mind with you at all times; of moving consciously through the world, instead of drifting.

For that is the key.

When you become aware, and learn to correlate cause and effect, you can see where any path is likely to lead you.

When you gain the courage to look honestly at the path ahead, and not try to fool yourself or others, then you will be able to choose wisely.

And when you are wise, and honest, and moving with kindness and firm intent through the world, then you have power indeed. Not power to force others, for that is as unethical as it gets, as you will see. But the power to change yourself and the world around you.

For oh yes, we can do magic.

And how well our magic works depends on the depth of our understanding and honesty.

Your magic will work because you say it will work, and you know with unshakable knowledge that your word is good, and you would not say it if it was not so.

So it all comes back to that basic honesty.

Remember what honesty means?

Now comes the hard part.

If I was here in flesh and blood, actually talking to you instead of sitting in front of my computer typing these words with numb fingers on this cold January afternoon (I wonder why the heat in this room never works?) I would lead you gently through these exercises, and it would take months and months. As it is, my friend, I am going to write them all down here. Don't forget to read this entire book before you try them.

Some of them will hurt.

Don't do more than you think you can do at any one time.

Treat yourself gently. Be fair with yourself, and forgiving. Deal with your younger self as you would with a loved younger sibling (And don't forget that anything you are not doing right now this very instant was, in fact, done

by a younger self. We learn every moment that
we are alive.)

At the same time, be firm with yourself.
Force yourself to do all that you think you can
do.

And above all, be honest with yourself,
even if you don't yet have the courage or
strength to be honest with others. No one else
need read your answers.

I suggest that you write the questions and
your answers in a separate notebook. This way
you can take this same course again later,
when your answers have changed (and they
surely will.) You can also more easily lend this
book to others.

To a large extent, I am trusting you to be
your own teacher; so I am also giving you the
teacher's guide, and telling you what the exercises are for. Look for the answers deep within
yourself, and don't hesitate to call on your own
instincts or to ask the Lady for help. Unlike
me, She really is there.

1. Define honesty.

*This is to see if you read the chapter. Or
perhaps your definition disagrees with mine. If
so, why?*

2. The thing I am most likely to be dishon-
est with myself about is ...

(This is to diagnose your own greatest weakness. If you know what that is, you will be able to be on your guard against it. For instance, if you can't bear to think about how easily you get angry, and you are very likely to pass the blame for your anger to someone else, this exercise can show you that; then later when you are making a decision about a friend, you can say to yourself "I'm not deciding that Frank was irrational because I hate to admit I got angry, am I?")

3. When I am dishonest with myself it is usually because …

This is just another way to get at the same problems as the question above. If you still come up empty, or can't face it at all, try re-phrasing the question for yourself until you can. Don't forget to write down the question you actually asked as well as your answer.

4. I have no problem being honest with myself about …

This is to find your strongest point. When you are building self-honesty, especially if you have grown up in a dishonest or manipulative environment, it is a good idea to build on your strength.

For example, if you are accustomed to being honest with yourself about how you feel about the food you eat, you can learn to expand that to being honest with yourself about how you feel about your home, and so on to being honest about your feelings in general, your environment in general, what makes you have those feelings, and so on.

Just remember not to try to take it too quickly or too slowly.

If you try to do too much at once, your defenses will come up. It may be way too dangerous to examine your feelings about your home, for instance; you may realize at a subconscious level that if you do that, it will inevitably lead to the realization that you have to get out of there. In that case, you will feel your mental blocks come up, and your brain will shy away to thinking about something safe and neutral. If it does, go with it for awhile; and then try to honestly examine how you feel about the seasons, or something like that. Don't let yourself get away with not trying anything new at all; but don't force yourself to go for the hardest thing straight away either.

If you do the first, you are likely to remain at this point on the path indefinitely. (Or at least until the Gods find it necessary to hit you on the head with a metaphorical 2X4 to get your attention.)

If you do the last, the chances are that the blocks will be so strong that you will decide that this is a stupid book, set it aside, and never finish the course.

5. I can talk to anyone honestly about...

Another phrasing of question 4. See the note for question 3, above.

6. At the moment, I would rate my self-honesty as ___ on a scale of 1 to 10, with 1 being constantly lying to myself, and 10 being completely and objectively honest with myself.

This is to see where you think you stand right now. I know this may be new to you, but this is another place where you really have to be honest about your honesty!

7. I would give myself this rating, because ...

This gives you a place to explain your thinking when you were answering the previous question. We don't want any pat answers here. The newer you are at this self-examination stuff, the longer this should take you. If you gave yourself a rating of 8.6, this is where you should explain to yourself why you chose that number. Do you miss a ten because you lie to yourself about your diet? Or because you know that you are fooling yourself about your relationship with your girlfriend? There is a lot of room here to find out a whole lot about yourself.

8. In a year, I would like to be ___ on this honesty scale.

This is goal setting. It gives you something to look back on in a year and decide if you were unrealistic about your goals and set them too high or too low. Goal setting is also part of this whole Craft stuff, so the practice will be good for you.

9. I am trying for this much progress because...

This is for you to explain yourself to the self who will be reading this a year from now, and may not remember why you thought that such a high number was a reasonable goal, or why you thought that you couldn't go any faster than that!

10. Honesty is important because...

This is the hard question. In this case, I am not as interested in whether you read the chapter as in how you think it will relate to your own life.

In other words, don't just repeat my words. My life is not your life, and I don't have all the answers; just some of them that work for me. I am afraid, my dear, that you will have to find your own. I am not a guru, (I am way too fond of chocolate, for one thing,) and I don't believe that my point of view is the One True and Right Way. In fact, I think that that attitude is what

is wrong with most organized religions. (The religion I espouse is decidedly disorganized!)

So write down your own reasons why honesty might be important to you. Or why you think it might be too dangerous, for that matter, or whatever it is you actually think.

This is self-exploration, after all.

CHAPTER 3 - SELF

Anyone else is just as important as I am.
I am just as important as anyone else is.
– Lady Miriel.
                   Livingtree Book of Shadows

When I was a very little girl, about three years old, my parents sent me to Daily Vacation Bible School at our church. I loved it. I knew that I was the prettiest and smartest little girl there, and the sun shone every day just for me, and everything that happened was for my own special benefit.

Then one of the other little girls fell down and skinned her knee. There was blood, dirt and tears, and everyone deserted me, and ran to her. I was annoyed, and demanded that my favorite teacher come back, and look at the picture I was drawing.

"I can't right now," I was told. "Shelly fell and hurt her knee."

I did a quick check, and felt perfectly fine.

"But it doesn't hurt." I objected.

"It doesn't hurt *you*. It's Shelly's knee. It hurts *her*."

And it struck me like a bolt between the eyes. Shelly's knee hurt her! Other people felt things that I never felt at all! Not just Shelly, but all the other kids, and all the teachers, and everyone I had ever met on the street or in the grocery store, and all the actors on Captain Kangaroo, and all the children in places like China that I would never, ever meet. Everyone, everywhere, was the main character in their own story, and I would never feel what they felt, or know what they knew, or see what they saw unless they told me!

In that moment, I realized that everyone I would ever see was just as alive as I was. That they were separate and distinct from me, that they were perfectly real, not there for my benefit at all. That every one of them had their own hopes and fears, their own dreams and goals, and that every one of them mattered.

That everybody was as important as I was.

For a moment I was paralyzed with the knowledge.

Then I ran to Shelly and asked if they would like me to get water in a cup and some paper towels to help clean her up.

Twenty-seven years later, after decades of trying to help everyone else whatever it cost me, six years into a bad marriage, and five years after I became initiated into the Craft, I achieved Third Degree.* And as so often

---

*If you don't know what this means, please read the Appendix.

H

happens during initiations and elevations my
perception of the world changed overnight.
Doors opened in my mind, and I suddenly
realized, like a bolt between the eyes, that I
was not the least important creature that the
Lady had ever created. That I had my own
feelings, and my own hopes and dreams and
aspirations. That I was just as alive and mattered just as much as anyone that I had ever
met.

That I was as important as anyone else.

For a moment I was paralyzed with the
knowledge.

Then I told my husband that there were
going to be some changes.*

And so I learned about the balance point.

Balance.

Center.

The spot where all the possible outcomes
on one side of a decision are weighed against
all the possible outcomes on the other side,
and they come out even.

Once you know where the balance point is,
you can choose the side that has the outcome
you desire.

If you don't know where the balance point
is, the best you can do is hope that when it
tips, it will tip in the direction you want.

---

*In the event, he had liked me better before, and a
year and a half later he walked out of my life. That was very
painful; but not as bad as daily sacrificing myself on the
altar of his ego. (The worst part was that I am sure that he
had no idea I was even doing that!)

For many decisions, you will strive to keep the balance intact.

Other decisions you will want to tip to one side or the other of the ledger, where you perceive the most good to lie.

But good for whom?

I warned you that this wasn't going to be easy.

This society basically produces a characteristic "selfness" continuum. At one extreme are those who think they are the only important person. At the other, those who think they are the only *un*important person. This is when you need to practice a little of the honesty that we spoke of in the last chapter, and decide for yourself where you stand.

You may still think that you are the only "real" person in the world, and that everyone else is merely a character in your story. They may have important roles or bit parts, but they basically don't exist except when you need them. It pays to stay on the good side of those in power over you, because they can do good things for you or cause you pain and problems. People who are under you, though, don't really count at all. They are only there for your convenience, and you can use them however you see fit to further your own goals. You may do this through ordering them to obey you, through manipulation, or through confrontation, whichever is the easiest for you, and the most likely to be successful. It's not important,

since they aren't important, and what they think of you is not important. Your Ego has not yet grown out of your Me. We will call this extreme the Mego.*

The other extreme is exactly the opposite. If you are one of these, you realized at some point that everyone else is real, and that what they want is vitally important. You were probably taught to think of the other person first at all times, and told that you were a "Good Girl" whenever you did. You think that anything you do for yourself is selfish, and feel guilty for doing it. You may go so far as to punish yourself for days for doing even a small thing that only you benefit from, even if it doesn't bother anyone else in the slightest. It's quite likely, if you are in this camp, that you find it impossible to believe that anyone else at all really likes you. Actually loving you is out of the question. After all you don't even love yourself. Which is good, isn't it? I mean, loving yourself is selfish, isn't it? And Good Boys and Girls are never selfish. You have spent years squashing every hope and dream you ever had, so that you

---

*In this discussion, I am using the terms "Mego" and "AntiMego" to illustrate my point, as a sort of mental shorthand, so that I don't have to say "People who are not sure of the reality of other people" or "Folk who think everyone else is more important than they are" all the time. I coined these terms for you to use to determine your *own* position on this scale; *not* someone else's.

As a general rule, labels that allow you to place others into a convenient box and then dismiss them are not honest, loving, or ethical.

could do what someone else wanted you to do. We will call this extreme AntiMego.

Of course, pure extremes are difficult to find. Most people fall somewhere along this cultural continuum, and have some of the Mego and some of the AntiMego characteristics. If you are in this group, you think that some people, say those who work in that insurance office you are currently fighting with, aren't real, and it doesn't matter what you say to them over the phone. After all, you have never met them, and they are giving you a considerable amount of grief. Other people, like your friends and family, are much more important to you than you are yourself, and your spouse's every whim is your command, because his opinion of you is of paramount importance. If you are in this group you probably have some encounters when you don't care in the slightest what those other people think of you, and some when you would do anything to have them like you, but don't think that they do.

You will act either as a Mego or an Anti-Mego, depending on the situation.

You will have to be honest with yourself here, and decide in which situations you take which roll.

It's also likely that you have AntiMego tendencies for just so long, and then something "snaps" and you may find yourself acting like a Mego!

Or perhaps you see your worth as being equivalent to that of any three other people. If only one or two want something you don't want, you don't have to take their needs into consideration. If three or four do, then their opinion outweighs yours.

You know your own situation. I don't.

The problem is that all of these are not realistic, not honest, not balanced.

In order to find the balance point, you must realize that you are as important as any *one* of the other people. Not as *all* of the other people, mind you, just as any one. We are not created equal, thank the Gods. There are multitudes of differences between us. But in order to be ethical, and to make clear choices about life, you need to realize that we are all created equally important.

Let me explain this graphically.

Look at the picture. The white end of the scale (number 0) is the Mego extreme. The black end (number 10) is the AntiMego. Most people fall somewhere in between, and their reactions for different situations are different. However, they tend to be consistent for that situation until they are pushed too far. Then they usually over-react, and flip-flop over the scale using 5 as the flopping point.

For instance, your normal reaction to your kids may be 9, meaning you would do almost anything for them, and nearly always put their needs ahead of your own. They know this, of course, and take advantage of it, and use you until finally you have had *enough!* At that point, your reaction suddenly becomes a 1. Even reasonable needs are no longer tolerable. The closer you get to one extreme, the closer you fall to the other when you snap. (Such snapping is only temporary, of course; but it is real.)

Our goal is to step off the continuum alto-gether, toward the balance point shown as A. This is not on the continuum; so there is no "snap." Very few of us, of course, have actually reached it. (After all, we were raised in this culture, too.) But, as you can see, as you approach the balance the extremes are off the ends of the scale you are now working with.

At M, for instance, you cannot fall lower than 2.2, or higher than 7.8.

H

Your self-image, then, will be an average of how you react on the continuum, modified by your letter; with Z being the continuum itself.

A perfectly balanced person would be 5A.

An absolute Mego is ZeroZ.

The most extreme AntiMego is TenZ.

You may be currently operating at something like 6.4L. This may vary from day to day, or even from hour to hour.

But the goal here is to treat yourself with the same consideration you would treat anyone else, and to treat anyone else with the same consideration you treat yourself, because you know that all of us are equally important.

The best way to get a handle on this is to pretend that you are not in the equation at all.

An example.

Say that your place on the continuum is at the AntiMego end. You are lactose intolerant, and if you eat ice cream you will be ill. You and a group of your friends have gone to a movie, and afterwards everyone else decides that they want to go to Snookies Ice Cream for a treat. You have been there before, and you know that they don't have anything but ice cream there. What do you do?

As an AntiMego who has not begun to study, you go to Snookies without saying anything, order an ice cream cone because you don't want anyone else to notice that you aren't having a good time, eat it with a cold

coil of dread in your stomach and a smile on your face, and spend all night being sick.

Now pretend for a moment that you are not the one who is lactose intolerant, it's Harvey. Do you have any problems with finding a solution now? Probably not. If it were Harvey, you could probably say to the group, "Oh! Harvey is lactose intolerant, and can't eat ice cream. Let's go to Farfel's instead; then we can all have ice cream, and he can get something else." Would you expect a lot of argument about this? No? Then next time, try saying, "Guys, if I eat ice cream I'll wish desperately that I hadn't by midnight. Mind if we go to Farfel's instead? Then you can all get ice cream and I can have something else." Chances are that they didn't even know you were lactose intolerant. If you get any grief at all, it's likely to be because you didn't tell them months ago, before they bought you that ice cream cake for your birthday.

Slightly different scenario. Let's say you are on the Mego end of the scale. Some friends have gone with you to the movies, and want to go to Snookies for Ice Cream afterwards. You don't like Snookies, because one of the salespeople was rude to you about a month ago. What do you do?

As a Mego who has not yet begun to study, going to Snookies is out of the question. You probably announce that you want to go to Farfel's, and your friends probably go along, even if they really had their hearts set on a flavor that they could only get at Snookies. After all, these people know you, and know just the kind of tantrum you are capable of pulling if you don't get your way. And that is how it should be, right?

Wrong.

As a Mego who is beginning to evolve, and find your way to a different kind of existence, lets run this without you even being there.

Six people have just gone to the movies and decide to go for a treat afterwards.

Five of them want to go to Snookies, because they have ice cream flavors there that they don't have anywhere else in town.

One of them is afraid that a waitress he doesn't like might be there.

Where should they go?

What should you do now? Still don't get it? Pretend you are one of the five. Ah! See how that works? Suddenly majority rules.

Remember. You are exactly as important as any one other person.

Next time, try going along with the majority. Perhaps the person who was rude to you won't be working that night! (Perhaps if she is, you should try being polite to her.)

As in any other personal development, though, you will only be able to change your image of your self if you really want to, and are willing to invest quite a bit of time and energy. Don't expect results overnight. Don't be discouraged if you find yourself sliding back into your old habits, especially if you are tired or ill. But do pull yourself back out of those old habits as soon as you realize that you are "backsliding!"

All of this is not to say that you must have a balanced self image before you can behave ethically. But it certainly helps.

In order to make sound ethical choices you will often find yourself weighing the possible outcomes that might come to you from a decision against the possible outcomes that might come to someone else. In such a situation, you must weigh yourself in the balance honestly and objectively. Knee jerk reactions favoring either yourself or others must be avoided.

We are not talking about harm here, mind you, but merely nuisance and inconvenience, or simply not getting what someone wants. Harm is another subject for another chapter. (See why you need to read the whole book?)

Now. Remember the folks at the insurance company? The ones that you felt free to act like a Mego with? Let's take a closer look at them.

That young woman on the phone is just as real, and just as important, as you are. She has her own hopes and dreams. And she is stuck in a job where she has to take grief on the phone all day every day.

Pretend that is you if you are feeling Mego.

Pretend she is one of your friends if you aren't.

Basically, try to love her.

Feel a little sorry for her? She probably didn't dream about working the telephones in an insurance agency when she was growing up. Did she make the decisions about how much the insurance was going to pay? Probably not. Does she realize before she even calls you what you are likely to say when you find out? Probably so. Will taking out your disappointment on her change the decision of the management? Not a chance.

So how much will it cost you to be nice to her? How difficult to say, "Rats. I hate it when things like this happen, don't you?" Wait for her reply. She probably isn't used to dealing with folk who treat her like a person. Then ask who you should talk to next to appeal the decision. She will probably be more than happy to tell you. Ask if they get this kind of thing a lot? What usually happens? Talk to her as if she was a friend. Then thank her for her time and help, and wish her joy in the rest of her day.

She will probably be so surprised that her whole outlook on her day will be changed. And she will probably be so relieved that you aren't yelling at her that she is likely to thank you for it, which will make you feel good. In any case, what could have been a really unpleasant experience will be made a good deal less painful for all simply because you

realized that she is a person, exactly as real as you are.

And the key to self image, and an honest, realistic view of others is simply love. You must learn to love yourself. You must learn to love everyone else. This doesn't mean that you make excuses for them, or that you don't see clearly when they are wrong. This doesn't even mean that you can't admit honestly to yourself or others that so-and-so is a jerk, or such-and-such a man is simply evil. It doesn't even mean that you have to give someone endless chances. There are times when enough is enough. It just means that you care for them anyway, and wish them to grow, and don't want to hurt them for anger or vengeance.

Practice by behaving with love toward strangers. That's much easier than loving that guy who is emotionally abusing your friend.

If you hold this always in your mind, harming none becomes second nature.

If you strive for this, you will leave good will, light, and laughter in your wake.

If you can achieve this, you will be very close to the Gods indeed.

OK. Exercise time. Remember what I said before the last set. (If you don't, go back and re-read it. It's on page 13.) All of that applies here as well.

1. On the Mego-AntiMego continuum, I feel that I usually act like ...

Honesty time again. Do some soul-searching and diagnose yourself accurately. If you are not accurate about this, then the exercises that you will do will be doing exactly the wrong thing. Don't decide that you must be a 1.4Y, because you left your entire family at home and went shopping by yourself the other night, and bought yourself the first new clothes you have had in the last year, and only got them Cinnabuns, and you have been feeling guilty about it ever since. The very fact that you are feeling guilty about it argues that you are not at that end of the continuum at all. Don't decide that you must be a 9.3W because you got your secretary a bunch of roses last Secretary's Day, and that was really very nice of you, wasn't it? The fact that you think that doing something fairly minor was really very nice of you argues against it.

2. I say that because ...

Here is the place where you explain your reasons for the type you chose above. Once again, please be honest and fair with yourself.

3. I want to change/don't want to change because ...

This is where you decide if you want to change your self image. Just because I think that staying on this continuum leads to unrealistic ethical decisions doesn't necessarily mean that you do. Perhaps you are perfectly happy being exactly what you are. In that case, tell me in no uncertain terms why you think that I'm way off target here. I would counsel you, though, that if you feel you are in perfect balance you should give yourself a few trail scenarios to check this out. I'm not doubting your word, dear friend, I just want you to be sure of yourself, and honestly honest with yourself.

On the other hand, maybe you do want to change your perception of yourself. In that case, tell me why. (Or to be more accurate, tell your own older self why. You will probably be rereading this someday. I probably won't.) What makes it important to you? What do you expect to gain by this change? What do you expect to lose from it?

4. An honest, balanced self image would include...

Here is your chance to get specific. What do you think you should be thinking about yourself? Remember, this is what you think; not what your parents told you, not what your teachers told you, not what I told you. Look inside, trust your instincts, and write down

what you tell you. You will know even as you write if you actually believe it or not.

5. **Write a list of your best character traits; those things that you would love if you found them in someone else. Make sure there are at least ten things on your list.**

This is primarily for the high numbers, those close to the AntiMego end of the scale: but it's a good idea for anyone to do it. Remember that this should be things you would like in someone else that you find in yourself.

I had a student once who said that the thing he thought others liked the most about him was that he was an authority in most subjects. The thing he liked the least in other people was that they thought they were experts in so many areas! At least he was right about his own perception of know-it-alls! Be honest with yourself, though. If you don't like a trait in others, there is an excellent chance that others won't be too fond of it in you!

You have to write down at least ten things, because you should learn to value your own good traits. There must be at least ten things about you that you would like in others, even if they are not strictly personality traits (ie. "I have nice hair," or "I am a good cook.") If you can think of more than ten, by all means write them down. Be honest and objective. Refer back

to this list when you are tempted to brutalize
yourself.

6. Write a list of things about yourself that
   you would like to change. Put no more
   than three things on your list.

This is primarily for those who recognize
themselves as having low numbers, on the
Mego end; but once again, anyone can benefit
from it. Here, do use things that are really personality traits. If you can only think of one
thing, then only write down one thing. The reason you are limited to three is that you can't
work on more than that at once anyway, and I
don't want to give you AntiMegos a chance to
beat yourselves up. You aren't perfect, and you
do need to change some things; but you don't
need to dig a deep pit, fill it with bungee sticks,
and fling yourself into it. If your mind fills with
stuff, pick three and write them down. Please
don't write down more than three anyplace! If
you just have to, then destroy your scrap paper
as soon as you finish writing down your three.
Once again, be honest, be fair, and don't expect
miracles of yourself (Not at this stage, anyway.)

7. If you pegged yourself at 3 or below, do
   something for someone else that can not
   possibly help you, every single day this
   week. If you are are 7 or above, do something for yourself that can not possibly

help someone else, every single day this week. If you are between 3 and 7, decide which of these exercises you would get the most good out of, and do that. Or do some of both!

This is to get you some practical experience in breaking out of your normal rut. You might be surprised with the results. I won't tell you what to expect, though; that would ruin the surprise.

8. See all the clerks, waitresses etc. that you encounter today as real people, with their own lives, and their own stories to tell. Really look at them. Acknowledge them as people.

This is really for folks nearer the Mego than the AntiMego end of the scale, but it will give you others something relatively easy and fun to do. It is also an important step off the scale entirely to begin to see that even the "little people" are really just the same as you and me. If you start talking to your waitress, for instance, you might be surprised at how interesting her life is when she isn't at work. I, personally, tend to ask folk to pose for me. This won't work for you unless you are an artist; but just being interested in someone else can work wonders for their day, and you can learn the most amazin' stuff!

9. Treat everyone sharing the road with you today as if they were real people in cars of their own, with destinations as important to them as yours are to you. If someone cuts you off in traffic, say a prayer for their safety and that of everyone they encounter as they hurry to their goal.

(My husband's reaction when I read this to him was "Lovely Lady, Laughing Lord, protect that fool and see him safely to his goal before he kills someone.")

The real reason for this exercise, of course, is to learn not to hate the people you share the road with. It's my opinion that a lot of accidents could be avoided if everyone assumed that the guy in the next car had a reason for behaving that way, and didn't get annoyed and try to get back at him. This is presupposing that the guy in the next car hasn't been drinking, of course. And if you drink and drive, just think next time of all the harm that you could easily do (and will, inevitably, do if you continue) just because you are too proud to admit that you have a little problem here. Should someone die for the sake of your pride?

10. Do something spectacularly nice for someone in your family, just to surprise them. If you rated yourself as an 8.5 or

above, then the person in your family to "treat" is you!

This exercise is here because it is often easiest to overlook people in one's own family, and not to see them as separate from oneself. In order to have an honest and ethical view of the world, it is absolutely necessary to realize that you are responsible for all of your own actions, and only your own actions; what your husband, your wife, your siblings, your parents, or your children do are the results of their own choices. You cannot control them in the slightest; and except in the case of your children, you shouldn't even try. The others are all grown-ups in their own right, unless you are a minor with minor siblings, in which case it is up to your parents to control them. It's not your job, man.

Even with children, you can show them what to do by word and example, you can bribe them, you can punish them, you can coax them or cajole them; but what they do, they will do because they have decided to do it. If they decide to ignore you, they will suffer the consequences of their own decisions. And that is hard. Oh boy, is that hard. I would do anything to protect my own children, to give them the instant benefit of all my years of experience, to keep them from ever getting hurt learning all the things they will have to learn. But that is not the way the world works. They have to make their own mistakes, and learn from them, and worst of all, I have to let them. They belong not to their father (unless they have been very bad. No, just kidding.) or to me, but to themselves.

The importance of not lumping your family in the same spot on the scale as yourself cannot be overemphasized.

You should treat them as well as you would treat your friends.

Doing something spectacularly nice for one of them every once in a while will show them how you value them. And that's very important for everyone.

CHAPTER 4 - LOVE

*If you love the Gods, you need to love all
people, because you need to keep in mind
that all people are aspects of the Gods, yourself included.*
   –Lady Minivah, of Livingtree Coven

Love.

We touched on this in the last chapter, but
now we are going to go into more depth on
the subject.

The word conjures up different pictures for
different people. It's a common word; often
used with little meaning (I love apples,) sometimes with great passion (I love chocolate.)
(No. Just kidding. No! I mean, I really *do* love
chocolate; but this is still the same kind of
usage. It simply denotes a preference for a particular food.)

For some people, love and sex are so inter-
twined that they are virtually synonymous.
(These folk love cucumbers.) (Sorry. I couldn't
resist. I can only take just so much seriosity at
once.) If someone tells one of these folk that
they love them, they expect to have sex soon.

H

Some people see love as a trap. Most of these were raised in abusive households, where they were told over and over "I'm doing this because I love you" while they were being brutalized. These people are afraid of love. If someone tells one of these folk that they love them, they expect to be hurt.

Some people see love as a manipulative device. They were raised in homes where they often heard, "If you really loved me, you would do this for me." They look on love with suspicion, or use it as a lever themselves. If someone tells one of these folk that they love them, they expect to be used.

Some people see love as a call for self-sacrifice. They think if you love someone, you have to give up everything for them. They either seek love as an unassailable reason never to do any thinking for themselves again, or fear it as a total annihilation of the self. If someone tells one of these folk that they love them, they flat don't believe it. They know no one is going to give up everything for *them*.

Some people see love as a call for others to sacrifice to them. They think if someone loves them, they will gladly give up everything for them. (If this is you, guess what personality category from Chapter 3 you fall into?) They look everywhere for love, seeking to find someone to take total care of them, and give them their undivided attention. If someone

tells one of these folk that they love them, they expect absolute dedication and enshrinement.

Some people see love as a colossal risk. They think if they love someone, they will be totally vulnerable to that person; and they have a difficult time trusting anyone quite that much. If someone tells one of these folk that they love them, they are filled with fear. What if they are expected to reciprocate? Better break off the relationship now.

Some people see love as a contract. They think if they love someone, the other person is required to love them. There will be a certain percentage split in things demanded and things given (the percentage depending on their own personality.) If the percentage is violated, then the contract is null and void. If someone tells one of these folk that they love them, they start expecting their percentage.

Some people see love as a commitment. They think if they love someone, they will have to be devoted to them for all time. They look for love as a safe and secure haven, unshakable by any force. If someone tells one of these folk that they love them, they expect that person to want to move in.

And there are thousands of other definitions and shades of meaning and connotation in that tiny little four letter word.

It would be impossible to love everyone with any of these definitions of love. You can't give everyone your undivided attention. You

can't even give *any*one your undivided attention – bodily functions, at least, will always
take up a certain amount of time. You can't be
with everyone all of the time, your house simply isn't that large! None of the abusing or
using definitions will do at all; the whole point
of the Ethics of the Art is to avoid using or
abusing people.

The sort of love that I'm talking about here
isn't even a feeling, although the feeling may
come in time. You can't force your emotions to
do something, any more than you can force a
cat to drink water. You can try, but is the tribal
scarring really worth it?

The sort of love I'm talking about is a verb.
It is the action of putting yourself into the
other person's place, and looking at them from
their point of view. It is the decision to give all
that you can honestly give without begrudging
it, whenever you are asked. It is the desire to
see them reach their full potential. It is a wish
that they find what they want in life, and attain
happiness.

This is not easy. But it is not impossible.

We are going to break this down one bit at
a time now.

First, the action of putting yourself into the
other person's place, and looking at them from
their point of view.

I have a dear friend and former student
(she is long graduated now) whose tastes in
almost everything are exactly the opposite of

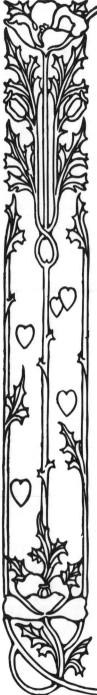

mine. I like things that are shades of blue, green, and violet with the occasional bit of red for accent. My favorite neutral color is white. I like winter, and snow, and cold, and frost on the ground. I heat my home to 65°, because I am uncomfortable if it is much warmer than that. I really enjoy the weather known as "bleak," when it's drizzly and windy and the temperature is in the sixties. I enjoy most other weathers as well, naturally. Cool sunny days are glorious! But too much sun hurts my eyes and makes my head ache. I can't tolerate spicy foods at all; in that department, I am decidedly a wimp. I am fond of plants, and have a houseful.

Her favorite colors are all in the red, yellow, and orange range. Her favorite neutral is brown. She likes hot, dry weather, and heats her home to 75° when she feels that she can afford it (We both live in Michigan.) She loves a type of decoration that can only be described as "gaudy." I think she's a bit ashamed of that taste; but she loves it nonetheless. She suffers from SAD; which means that short days and long nights cause a chemical imbalance that makes her depressed. She has to sit in front of strong lights to counteract this. She loves spicy foods, and can eat stuff that makes my eyes water across the room. She can't grow any plants except aloe. She's allergic to most others. (I'm allergic to aloe!)

But we have no problems being friends.

See, when I buy her a gift, or do something for her, I keep her tastes, her likes and dislikes in mind. I would never buy her a lovely blue vase with a subtle snowflake pattern, although I might be enormously taken with it myself. For her, I would buy a brown box, embellished with gold and set with a striking pattern of red glass jewels and amber.

And this is reciprocal. She also keeps my taste in mind when buying things for me.

Do you understand?

When I am doing something for her, I pretend that I *am* her, and I look at things the way she would look at them.

But that is relatively easy, dealing with tastes and likes and dislikes. It's surface stuff.

You also need to love people on the deeper levels.

You need to put yourself in the place where their fears and hopes and dreams grow.

You need to understand that theirs are not the same as yours.

Another example.

Say you have a challenging job that pays quite well. You enjoy it enormously, and look forward to every single day. But you have a good friend whom you see as stuck in a dead-end job doing boring filing work for only slightly above minimum wage. He seems quite content there, but you know he could do better. An opening comes up in your company, doing basically the same thing you do, with

on-the-job training, great pay, and loads of
benefits. You are sure he could do the job, and
you are sure that you could get it for him.
What should you do?

Ask him if he is interested. Paint it in glowing terms if you want, tell him you will be right
there to help if he's wary, offer your expertise
until he is used to the situation; but only offer.
He may really like the job he has. He might
know that if he is under stress he is likely to
start drinking again, a problem that he over-
came long before you met him. He might see
your job as one long string of crises, and know
that he doesn't function well in a crisis.
Perhaps your job would necessitate a long
commute, and he knows that he gets terribly
carsick if he is in traffic for more than twenty
minutes. Maybe he really intends to be a
writer, and is working on a book at home,
using the long boring hours at his day job to
think out characters and develop plot lines. A
job like yours would take way too much time
away from what he sees as his real job. He
might know from bitter past experience that
your job would give him an ulcer in less than a
month. There are hundreds of possible reasons
why he might not be interested.

And the kicker is that he might not want to
discuss his reasons with you.

Put yourself in his place. Would you want
to tell someone you admire that you can't possibly apply for his job, because if you do your

prison record will come up? Or even that you can't do his job, because if you try to talk to more than one person at a time, you know you will stutter? Or that you know that his boss is a homophobe, and even though you are still deeply in the closet you are, in fact, gay?

Allow your friends their privacy.

Allow them their own lives.

Never force them to do something because you think it would be "good for them."

Never, never assume that something would be good for someone else because it would be good for you.

There are billions of people on this planet, and every single one of them may travel hundreds of paths in their lifetime. Dear friend, please understand that the odds of meeting anyone in exactly the same spot on exactly the same path as you are vanishingly small. Each person is an individual case, and must be treated as such.

Please, please remember this.

Love is the decision to give all that you can honestly give without begrudging it, whenever you are asked.

Now there is a sentence for you.

Honesty we have covered in a previous chapter, but what in the world do I mean by "without begrudging it?" Do I mean that you are supposed to suppress your feelings of resentment? No. What, then, you aren't supposed to have any at all? How can you manage that?

Simple. By not giving anything you cannot afford to give.

Let me explain.

I was raised to be a good Christian. By my parent's definition, (besides being obedient, which was the primary thing) this meant I was expected to pour out my life-blood for others, as Christ poured out his life-blood for us. Give till it hurts, and all that.

But I am no longer a Christian; good, bad or otherwise; and I have learned not to pour out my life-blood. I need it to sustain my life, and I can do a lot more for a lot more folk if I am alive and in reasonably good health.

If you give until it hurts, it hurts; and you end up resenting someone or something for it.

On the other hand, when you begin to give what you can afford to give, you find that the three fold law is in effect here. Remember the three fold law? Anything you do comes back to you three-fold. Tripled. Anything, for good or ill!

So when you give out of a sense of duty, and your gift is given in resentment and tainted with despair, what you get back is enough to sustain you, but it's given grudgingly, out of duty, and the givers are likely to let you know every few minutes that they gave it to you, and you owe them.

But what you give from your bounty, in a sense of joy and friendship, comes back to you with three times the joy and friendship attached!

Do you understand?

If you feel that your resources have been stretched as far as they will go, everyone is much better off if you freely admit that; especially if you know someplace else the person who needs help can go for it, and tell her about that place.

When what you are giving requires energy, like healing, scrying, or magic, remember not to give your own. If you do, you will someday encounter someone who needs all of it, and you will be burned out just like that. Instead, learn to channel energy from the Earth. If you don't know how to do that, then please, please don't do this kind of work at all until you learn.

Only give what you can honestly give.

People will understand.

Love is the decision to give all that you can honestly give without begrudging it, whenever you are asked.

Giving, helping others, is such a long and complex subject that the whole next chapter is devoted to it. But we will touch briefly on it here.

Helping "whenever you are asked."

Not interfering unless they request help is the key.

Remember when you were young, and your parents or older siblings were showing you how to do something? Remember that they would keep on showing you long after you thought you understood what they were getting at? Remember how frustrated you used to get? How you used to tell them, "I want to do it myself! Let me do it!!"

Well, helping others is a lot like that.

Don't, unless they ask for help.

Then give them exactly the help they ask for.

You see, my friend, ultimately we are not the teachers here, the Gods are. We have no way of even knowing what the lesson is supposed to be, although we can guess.

It is vitally important to let people have the freedom to allow their own higher selves to pick the lessons, even though it often means that we have to stand in frustration with our hands in our pockets, not giving aid because they don't want it.

Remember the child? If your parents hadn't said, "Alright." and let you try your hand, would you ever have really learned? Would you not eventually have given up, and stopped even trying to learn? Would you not eventually have expected to have everything done for you as a matter of course?

People learn from their mistakes. Some folk would even argue that people learn best from their mistakes. Part of loving people is

allowing them to make mistakes. Even disastrous, easily avoided mistakes.

Advise them, by all means.

Point out the path they are on, and where you think it will lead.

Offer to help them in any way you can.

Jump up and down, wave your arms around and shout "Warning! Warning! Danger, Will Robinson!" if you feel you must.

But unless they are children, legal minors under your care and responsibility, or have been declared mentally incompetent and legally placed in your care, you must not grab them and fling them off the path they are on.

It is their path, not yours.

It is their life, not yours.

Their mistakes are their own responsibility, not yours.

Their lessons are their own lessons, not yours.

Remember, I never told you this was going to be easy.

(Besides, you might be wrong about the danger. Very few of us are infallible. I, at least, have never met anyone who is.)

Love is the desire to see people reach their full potential.

As you may already know, I am an artist by profession and inclination. As such, I have many friends who are artists as well. Most of my friends, like me, will help any budding

artists that we encounter. But not all artists will.

Some seem to think that if someone comes along who is more talented, they will lose their job. They treat all the tricks of the trade like secrets. (Well, so do we, actually. But in our case, that means that we tend to say, "Shhh. Don't tell anyone. It's a secret." before we explain a particular technique to an entire roomful of folk who have come to hear us speak at a panel.) It doesn't matter to these few what happens to the young artist; they are only concerned with themselves. I have even heard them quite actively trying to discourage the up-and-comers, telling them they have no talent, and will never make it in the field when one glance at their sketchbooks tells quite the opposite story.

I find this behavior unethical on several counts. Not only is it dishonest, and fairly brutal; they are purposely trying to stunt the growth of another person.

We don't do this.

We foster growth.

It's quite possible that someday one of the kids that I have helped into this field will land a job I wanted. Freelancing is like that. It's even possible that the kid will land all the jobs I want, although I doubt it; there seems to be more than enough work to go around.

The point is; that doesn't matter.

If she does get the job instead of me, then at least in the opinion of the art director, she was better suited for it.

What matters is that I helped her all I could, and she is reaching her full growth, and there is more beauty in the world because of it.

None of us will last forever in this incarnation.

It is up to us to foster growth in everyone around us, so that those who come after us will stand straighter and taller than we did.

And the next time round, they will help us to grow, in turn.

You must also leave people free to grow at their own pace, and bloom into their own flower.

You can't make a rose bloom faster by peeling back the petals; you just get a dead rose that will never bloom.

Neither can you force a person to grow more quickly than they are meant to grow. You just get a bruised and battered soul that may take lifetimes to heal.

Do you understand, dear friend?

Even someone who is a real jerk can grow. (Especially someone who is a real jerk can grow. There is so much room for growth there!) You cannot force them to grow if they don't want to, and you are not required to stand there and support them forever if they won't take that first step, but you must not try to suppress their growth, even if you don't like

the direction that it is taking, unless it is going to harm someone else. (That is a special case, and we will discuss it later in the book.)

So love people. Put yourself in their place, and foster their growth; don't knowingly hinder it.

Love is a wish that the other person will find what they want in life, and attain happiness.

This is the easy one. It's relatively simple to wish someone good, for wishing takes very little work. And yet, it is important, too. As trivial as a wish might seem, in order to make it, you have to be standing in a certain relationship to the wishee. He has to occupy a certain direction in your world view. You wouldn't wish someone ill if you loved them. Likewise, it is almost impossible to sincerely wish someone good if you hate them.

In order to wish them well, you have to change your own viewpoint toward them.

You have to change to a position of loving them.

You have to smile at them.

And they will feel that you wish them well.

That is why this is important.

Not to mention that everything you do for good or ill comes back to you three times, remember? Think how many well wishes that is for you!

One more word of caution. Remember the beginning of this chapter, when we discussed some possible ways people might react if someone told them they loved them? Well, all of that is still true. The only person you are changing here is you. What do you do about that?

The answer is really simple. If you think that they could not possibly understand what you mean by saying "I love you," then don't say it.*

OK. Now for the exercises. As before, please read the whole book before you do any of these. And if you don't remember the instructions in Chapter 2, please go back and re-read them now. They are on page 13.

1. When someone tells me they love me, I think they mean ...

This is the beginning of the diagnostic section of this chapter. In order for you to understand what is meant by love, and what honestly loving someone is all about, you first have to be clear about what you mean by love. Remember the examples at the beginning of the chapter. Describe what it means to you in detail; include your hopes, fears, expectations, dreams, everything. Be honestly honest with yourself. Some of this may be fairly unrealistic.

---

*The exception, of course, is family members. Tell them anyway. Society approves of this, so they will probably get used to it. What I mean is, it's probably not a good idea to tell your boss, or that waiter, or the bus driver.

You may be able to see that the moment you begin to write it down. I had a friend once who, when she examined what she meant by someone loving her, realized that what she expected was a knight on a white charger to come rushing up and rescue her from a bad situation she was in. As soon as she saw this, she exclaimed that she hated damsels in distress that sat around waiting to be rescued. Less than a month later she had rescued herself.

2. I react to this by ...

More diagnostics. Some folk will tell you that you should be acting, not reacting; but that is unrealistic in my opinion. You don't want all your actions to be reactions, but some of them are bound to be. The trick is to know which are which. You almost certainly feel something, probably both physical and emotional, when someone unexpectedly tells you they love you. If you know what that reaction is, then if someone evokes it you will know that that is simply your normal reaction to this phrase and not necessarily your reaction to the situation. By the same token, if you answered the question above in glowing, rosy terms, but when you picture someone actually saying this your immediate reaction is to run away, then you know that you have a dichotomy here that you will need to work on.

3. When I tell someone I love them, I usually mean …

Still more diagnostics. This question will let you know if you expect the same thing from other people that you expect from yourself. If the difference here is great, then you know that you need to closely examine your definitions. Looking at it honestly, it becomes obvious that you are being unrealistic somewhere here.

4. I expect them to react by …

Basically the same as above. Are the reactions you expect the same as the reactions that you have? If they aren't, you will need to do some serious self-examination until you know why not.

5. I have no trouble believing that others love me. T/F

A simple true/false question. If you have trouble answering it, you probably should answer "false." People who have no trouble believing that people love them have no trouble believing that people love them; of course people love them. What a silly question!

6. This is because …

Ah. Time for some real soul searching here. I, personally, had a great deal of trouble believ-

ing that other people could possibly love me. *If* they said they did, they were obviously just being kind, or they thought it was the socially required thing to do. You might even say that I was sure to the bottom of my heart that people could not possibly love me. Then my husband (my current husband, not the one who walked out) asked me why I wanted to feel that way. My first reaction was that it wasn't a question of wanting to feel that way. I simply felt that way! But, being honest with myself, I had to admit that everything I did I did because I chose to do it. Therefore, I was, in fact, choosing to believe that I was unlovable. Why? The simple, pat answer was that I didn't love myself; but that was not only too simple, too much what I had been told my whole life, but also not even true. I did love myself. I just didn't want to even think about other people loving me. I preferred to think that if I fell off the face of the planet no one would even miss me. And then I had it. I had chosen to believe that no one loved me at all, because if they did then I had an obligation to be there for them. I didn't want anyone loving me, because I didn't want the responsibility.

Of course, as soon as I realized that, I also realized that whether I thought I wanted the responsibility or not, I sure had chosen to put myself in a place where it was all mine. After all, I chose to marry my husband, and I knew I would have instant kids when I made that

choice. Not to mention choosing to have students, lead a coven, and so on.

What I am trying to tell you with this whole long-winded example is that whatever you feel, you feel because at some level you choose to feel it. Your reason for that choice may not be as selfish as mine was; but it was your choice.

What you need to do here is find out the reasons behind that choice. And don't be surprised if a year from now you find you can dig deeper into yourself, and come up with reasons behind your reasons.

Once again, be honest with yourself; but don't force yourself to look into something you really, really don't want to examine. In that case, use the pat answer. It's OK. In time you will be able face anything.

I was in the Craft twelve years before I could face that particular thing about myself. I am still learning to make changes, and live with them. It's still a lot easier, at times, to fall back into the old, worn, comfortable habit of thinking I am totally unloved. The only problem is that now I know it simply isn't true!

7. I am comfortable/uncomfortable with this because …

This is where you can explain to your older self how you feel about the way you feel. I felt very uncomfortable about how I felt about people loving me, because it was immature and selfish, a mere avoidance technique that I set up to keep from feeling tied down. (Well, I am a double Sag after all.) I am still not totally comfortable with the way I feel about people loving me as I write this, because it's still a little new to me, and because I'm still a little wary about that tied down bit. (see above.) However, I'm getting more used to it daily; and in any case what I have now with my family and friends is exactly what I always wanted. I'm bound to them anyway, because this is the only place I want to be.

8. I want to change/don't want to change the way I think about love, because ...

More soul-searching. The same question, once more removed. If you like the way you think about love, this is easy. If you don't like it, but you want to change, it becomes harder. If you don't like it, and you don't want to change it may too hard for you to do. If that is the case, skip it. Write down the date, and a note that you are deferring this one, and come back to it when you can deal with it.

In fact, it's a good idea to do that with any exercise that you aren't ready for yet. Just as you wouldn't try to lift 300 lbs. the first day you sat down on the weight bench, it is dangerous to try to examine parts of your psyche that you aren't ready to look at yet. The difference is that it's easy to tell when something is 300 lbs. on the bench. In your mind, you have to let your instincts and feelings guide you. If you begin to sweat, or shake, or feel nauseated; or if your mind begins to race around in little circles looking for a way out, stop. Take a deep breath, and try something that you don't want to fight quite so hard.

9. When Robin tells us to love everyone, she means …

This is to see if you read the chapter, and to give you a simple, easy, straightforward exercise with no soul searching involved.

10. I think I can/don't think I can do this, because …

Back to the soul searching, I'm afraid. Look at this as your chance to note whether you think my expectations are reasonable or not. Pretend you are writing a letter to me, and tell me exactly what you think of my ideas. Later, when you re-read it in a year or so, see if you still agree then with what you thought now. Remember, all this growth stuff is an ongoing process. It never stops.

CHAPTER 5 - HELP

*"Helping someone doesn't mean taking
the control out of their hand and doing it for
them."*
   ~ Tim Short, age 11

Helping others.

Almost everyone wants to.

It's natural.

You see someone struggling with something you know you could easily do, and your first reaction is probably the desire to go over and offer to give them a hand.

If it wasn't, you probably wouldn't be reading this book; you would be the most self-satisfied and self-centered of Megos, and the whole concept of ethics would seem pointless to you.

The key, as I mentioned in the last chapter, is to offer.

And if your offer is refused, to stand aside and let them do it.

This doesn't mean that you have to walk out of the room.

You can even extend your offer. It's perfectly OK to say, "Well, if you change your mind, let me know."

It's not perfectly OK to breath down their necks, or point things out over their shoulders, or keep nagging them to accept your help.

It is flat wrong to take it from them, and do it for them.

It's just plain stupid to take it from them, do it for them, and then expect them to be grateful to you!

You see, my friend, people instinctively like to do things themselves.

At a very deep level, everyone realizes that doing stuff for themselves is part of the growing process. That without that sort of hands on manipulation, they will not learn the lesson they need to learn. There is also a great drive to be independent; to be able to take care of themselves. Not to mention that doing something yourself is the only way to be sure it will be done the way you want it done.

Watch a very small child sometime. They literally scream if you don't let them have the reins when they want them.

Somewhere along the line, though, this primordial instinct is changed.

Some of us are taught to wait patiently and let our parents show us many times, so they are sure that we will never make a mistake. We become afraid of trying until we are sure that we can succeed.

Some of us are basically ignored, and learn that we are completely on our own. We are shocked if someone offers to help, and don't have the slightest idea what to do with the offer. Asking for either permission or guidance is totally foreign to us.

Some of us are never allowed to try our own hands at all. We become used to having things done for us, and tend to just stand there looking blankly at the tools if we are expected to do something ourselves.

Some of us are given the chance to try as soon as we want it, and encouraged whether we succeed or fail. We tend to look at life as a series of challenges, and we enjoy challenges.

And these are just a few of the ways that we have been taught to react to help, and don't take into account the differences in the personalities we were born with.

When I was in my teens I used to take care of a little that had us all very worried. By her third birthday, she still hadn't said her first word. She seemed to understand us quite well; she just never said anything at all herself. Not Mama, not Dada, not Wawa, nothing. She was strictly a point, grunt, and nod kind of kid.

Then a few weeks after her third birthday, she began to speak. Not baby talk, mind you; speech. Her first sentence to me, when she had been verbal for less than two days, was, "You know, your nose-holes look just like footprints in the snow." Turns out that she had been practicing in secret for years. She just hadn't wanted to speak where anyone could hear her until she knew she had it down pat. (I found that out, because I asked her, and she told me.) She is a Harvard graduate now, and I suspect she still has the same outlook on life in general, and looking like a fool in particular.

The point is, people have different reactions to offers of help, and want different amounts of it.

Here, as in everything else, you must let the other person tell you what they want and need. Look at it from their point of view. Allow them to grow at their own pace.

I know I said a lot of this in the last chapter, but it bears repeating.

The most important thing is not to take over for them, not to do anything for them unless they ask you to.

If you do, you aren't helping at all. You are butting in.

It's not polite.

It's not responsible.

And it's not your job.

OK. You know this already. You are going to politely offer your help, and wait until they accept before you do anything. You even remember not to offer anything you cannot afford to give.

But they accepted your help. They want your help. They practically begged for it! Now what?

Now you do what they ask you to do.

I had a friend once who was always eager to help me. He constantly offered, without being pushy about it; but I only accepted his help once. You see, dear friend, when I said, "Yes," he took that as permission to take control. He totally ignored me, didn't pay any attention at all to what I wanted, and finished the whole project as if it was his own. Then he expected me to admire his work, and tell him I could never have done it without him.

Except that I had been looking forward to doing the project myself. I could have done it. It wouldn't even have been that hard. And when it was finished, I would have had what I wanted; not what he thought I wanted. All I actually wanted from him was directions on how to run the belt sander!

Do you see?

An offer to help should be an offer to be a consultant or an employee, not a boss.

If someone really asks you to just take over, because they are completely out of their depth, or need to go do something else, then, and only then, it is OK to treat it like your project.

It's nearly as annoying to have someone asking every few seconds, "You want it done like this, right?" when you have asked them to just do the job, as it is to have them take over, isn't it?

And after you are acting as consultant or employee, you should be the best consultant or employee you can be.

If what they need is information, then give

them the information they asked for as completely as you can. Don't ignore the directions for the belt sander, and tell them about the orbital sander instead. If you think they are about to make a mistake, it is perfectly alright to say, "I'll tell you about the belt sander if you really want me to, but I think the orbital sander will do a better job on that, because you don't want to sand the veneer completely off, just smooth it, right?" This will give them a chance to either ask you why the belt sander will take the veneer off, inquire what you mean by veneer, or tell you that, as a matter of fact, they hate this veneer and it's got to go! Don't make choices and decisions for them. Give them the advantage of your experience, but let them use it or ignore it as they will.

It's their life.

They are the ones that will be living with the consequences of their actions.

If you are acting as an employee, do what you are asked to do when you are asked to do it. Do it cheerfully (after all, you choose to offer to help here,) and finish the task. If you realize at any point in the process that the help you have been asked for exceeds the resources you can afford, let the person you are helping know that right away!

I find it incredibly frustrating to ask someone for help, or accept someone's offer of help, only to find that they are busy taking out the trash, which didn't need to be done, and which I never asked them to do, at just the moment when I really need them to drain the potatoes. Or worse yet, they are there when I ask them to drain the potatoes, but they wander off someplace between getting out the colander and taking the pot off the stove and are nowhere to be found!

If I ask someone to pick up the cookies and bring them to the gathering next Saturday, then I am expecting them to do that. I don't want to get there on Saturday and find no cookies because they realized after they got their paycheck on Friday that they couldn't afford to pick them up after all. I want them to call me on Friday as soon as they see they can't do it, and let me know, so that I can make other arrangements.

Do you see?

After your help has been accepted, it is extremely important to follow through. Do what you are asked to do, and only what you are asked to do. Finish the tasks you have taken on, or let it be known as soon as possible that you cannot. Advise, but don't direct unless you are asked to direct.

All these examples are for physical help; projects in a woodshop, getting food or parties together, stuff like that. The basic concepts are even more important when dealing with non-physical help.

Let's look at an example.

When someone's marriage is breaking up,

and they turn to you for help, it is incredibly important not to be officious; don't order them around, tell them what to do, take over, imply that you know exactly what is best for them. That isn't what they want. They probably just need someone to talk to while they sort out their own feelings, which are likely to be extremely mixed. They may need financial help, or a place to stay for a while. They may be really shy about asking for any of this; after all, they have just been completely rejected and betrayed by the person who was supposed to love them forever – how can they expect mere friends to care at all?

What you need to do is basically to be there. Be an ear, and a shoulder to cry on. If you have been through this, either for yourself or with another friend, and you know what to look out for, give them warnings and advice; "You really need to take his name off your AmEx card." "Please don't go back into the house alone. If he's there he is likely to hit you again." But be aware that they may not be ready to believe it's over, and may not be able to make the kind of move that signals this is really the end. Be aware, as well, that it may not *be* the end.

Call when you can, and see how they are doing; but don't nag or be a nuisance. I know this is a fine line to walk. But love them. Pretend you are them. (Completely different from pretending it's you in their place.) You

know the sort of person they are, right? You already know what they tend to see as interference and what they would probably view as concerned friendship. You probably even know whether concern makes them feel loved, or nervous! Act with that knowledge.

Offer them a place to stay if you like.

Don't be hurt if they go somewhere else instead.

They may be quite fond of you, but your "grundge levels" are too far apart.*

If they do move in with you, either explain when you offer that they can only stay for a limited period of time, and just how long that is, or be prepared to let them stay for as long as they need to.

If you decide after they are in your basement that this is not working out, and it's about to cost you your friendship, tell them. Tell them why. Emphasize that it isn't their fault, because they are hurting enough right now. Explain that you can't bear to lose the friendship because of incompatible grundge

---

*Grundge level is a technical term meaning the point at which you simply must drop everything else, no matter how important it may be, and clean your house. For some people this may mean when every single dish in the house is in the sink. For others it may mean when there is a pillow out of place on the chair in the living room. I have noticed over the years that people are uncomfortable in homes that have a grundge level significantly different than theirs, no matter which direction the difference takes. Folk are made as nervous by houses that are too clean for them as by those that are too messy. Once again, personal differences among different people. None of them are "right" or "wrong" unless the health inspectors come after you!

levels, for instance. Then help them to find
another place to go (not the same as finding it
for them unless they ask you to) and give them
a reasonable amount of time to move.
Otherwise, you are just compounding the
rejection.

If you don't think that you can do this,
then don't offer to let them move in in the first
place; and if they ask to, explain as gently as
you possibly can why they can't. You might try
to make a joke, if you think they would appre-
ciate a joke just now. "It wouldn't be prudent.
Not at this juncture." But make it a soft, gentle
joke, with nothing personal of any kind in it.
For instance, the joke above would suddenly
be cruel if the soon-to-be-ex was in the habit
of imitating past presidents.

Be careful with jokes. I used to make them
all the time, whenever things seemed too
tense or were cutting too close to the quick.
Then I found that several of my friends
thought I wasn't taking their problems seriously.
Far from helping, my attempt to get them to
laugh was actually making things worse.

Once again, as always, be honest, be loving, look at life through your friend's eyes, and
then do what you feel you should.

Also, don't hesitate in difficult situations
like this to ask the Lady what you should say.
You might be surprised at what wisdom will
suddenly come out of your mouth.

The next important thing to realize about

helping someone else is that your help may
never be reciprocated; at least not by them.

Don't expect it.

Don't demand it.

Don't keep a score card.

The threefold law will sort all of this out,
too. You can depend on it the way you depend
on gravity. You don't expect the things you put
down to just go floating off on their own, do
you? (Well, unless you work on the Shuttle or
something you probably don't.) Do you find it
necessary to get out the duct tape and velcro
to make sure the plates stay put when you set
the table? Or do you expect them to just lie
there unless they are interfered with by the cat?

It's like that.

If you are concerned with getting paid back
for your efforts, rest assured that you will be.

But the payment is not likely to come from
the same person you helped. You may not
even get paid back at all in this lifetime. You
may be saving up your "universal credits" so
that you can be born as a millionaire or a
musical prodigy in another lifetime, when you
intend to explore what that sort of existence is
like. Only the Gods and your Higher Self know
for sure.

You may even have a large debt to pay off
yourself, before you begin to accrue credits.

The point is, it will only make you crazy to
worry about it, and spend time and effort trying to make it all come out even, or assure a

balance in your favour. The universe will do
that all by itself anyway; so relax and let it.

Do you understand?

So; now you know all about giving good
help (it's so hard to get good help, you know),
and not expecting the person you help to be
able to help you back. What's next?

Next, my friend, is the real ethical buga-
boo.

When not to give help, even though it's
asked for.

You already know, of course, not to give
help if you cannot afford it.

But what do you do when you can afford
it, and the person is practically begging you for
it, but you feel, deep down, that it's time for
them to learn to stand on their own two feet?

You listen to your instincts.

Don't help if you can't afford it.

Don't help if they can't afford it, either.

If you are being honestly honest with yourself about their situation, if you are looking at
them with love, there will come a time when
you realize that doing this for them will stunt
their growth. At that time you need to explain
to them, as gently as they will hear you,* that
it is time for them to try this on their own.
That you feel they are ready, and that you are
no longer 'holding them up' as in supporting

---

*Sometimes they won't hear you unless you shout.
Start gently, and work up gradually to hitting them on the
head with the proverbial two-by-four to get their attention, if
you have to.

them, but 'holding them up' as in delaying them.

Once again, the fine line between being a help and being a hindrance.

Between showing them the way and carrying them on your back.

Just be absolutely certain that you are being honest, and refusing to help them out of love. If you are just tired of carrying them, simply tell them so, and let them decide if they are ready to walk. A six month old can't walk, no matter how heavy she gets. If your arms are aching, someone else must carry her. A two year old can walk by herself, but not for very long. She may be able to give you a break, but you will probably find yourself picking her back up soon. A ten year old can walk almost as far as you can, and shouldn't need any carrying at all. An eighteen year old can probably carry you if necessary!

Personal development follows the same pattern, but it's a bit harder to determine what age you are dealing with. Harder, but not impossible. If you look at the person with love and honesty, you can usually tell if you are dealing with a two year old who has gone as far as her little legs will carry her, or a lazy ten year old.

Again, don't hesitate to ask the Lord and Lady for guidance.

And if in doubt, go ahead and help.

It will do a whole lot less damage to carry

the ten year old than to leave the two year old abandoned at the side of the road.

Which brings us to the last thing you need to know about helping. For many of us, this may be the hardest part of all.

It's accepting help.

We all need help sometimes. There is nothing wrong with that at all. None of us can do everything perfectly the first time without any instruction whatsoever. If you expect to be able to, you are just fooling yourself, aren't you? And remember, we are being honest here, right?

You wouldn't feel ashamed of your friends if they asked for help, would you? Then what could possibly be wrong with you asking for it?

Do you think that everyone you know believes you to be perfect and infallible? Able to make perfect choices every time, to be everywhere at once, and to leap tall buildings in a single bound? No? Then why should they think less of you if you need help?

Even the Gods ask for our help, right?

Or is yours the opposite problem?

Maybe you don't think you are worth helping.

If that is the case, you know by now that I think you should do some work on your self image, don't you? (If you don't, please go back right now and re-read Chapter 3. Yeah. I thought you did.) I don't expect you to have an instant growth spurt in that department so that you immediately find that you deserve all the help you can get. But I also don't want you to suffer along in silence without asking for help for as many years as it might take to find that you are, in fact, as worthy of a little help as anyone else.

So try this, my friend.

It helps others to allow them to help you.

You can learn an awful lot by explaining something to someone else, can't you? The simple act of explaining forces you to clarify the subject in your own mind. The person you are explaining to often asks questions that act as catalysts, exposing parts of the process you hadn't thought about, and leading you to think in new and unexplored directions. Wisdom comes out of your mouth unbidden, and you learn new things from hearing it.

You are familiar with at least part of this, aren't you?

The best way to learn about something is to teach it.

The quickest way to become proficient at a task is to show someone else how to do it.

The friendliest way to pick up an entirely new skill is to give someone else a hand doing it.

Well, when you let others help you, it gives them the chance to teach, or show, or lend a hand. And this helps them to learn and grow.

Allowing your friends to help you also gives them a chance to earn "universal credits."

Not to mention that it can do wonders for their self-esteem; especially if they have been on the receiving end of a lot of help from you. Letting that eighteen year old lift you over a few rough spots really makes her feel strong, doesn't it?

Just don't make up work for them to help with, whatever you do. Honesty, remember? If you make stuff up so that they can feel needed they will probably be able to tell. Make work is not helpful to anyone. It's condescending, and arrogant, and assumes that they have nothing better to do with their time.

If there really isn't anything you need help with, let it go.

But if there really is, try asking for it; especially if that is difficult for you.

It shows a little vulnerability. It opens you up a bit, and lets some other folk in. It makes this friendship thing a two way street. It allows relationships to be reciprocal. And just the way that corrugated cardboard is stronger if the corrugations run in both directions, your friendships will be all the stronger for it.

Always, always, remember to thank the person who helps you, even if it isn't good help. If you don't like the way they helped, you might want to explain gently why it wasn't really help. If you don't feel comfortable doing that, or it wouldn't be socially acceptable in that situation, don't accept their help again. But please don't be rude. There is plenty of rudeness in the world without our adding to it. Treat them with love.

Just don't become a help junkie. Balance,
remember? The eighteen year old is going to
get awfully tired of you if you don't let her put
you back down! If you really need that much
help, maybe you should consider getting a pro-
fessional!

(OK, there's a bit of joke there, but I really
mean it too, dear friend. There are maid services listed in the yellow pages of most towns,
or check the classifieds under help wanted if
the problem is too much housework and not
enough time. There are temps available everywhere if you are running a business and the
problem is too much office work, and not
enough time. There are typing services, people
who will run you here and there for a small
fee, groceries can be delivered; check it out! If
you are disabled or have a limited income, you
can probably get special help for the things
you need. If, on the other hand, your problems
are not physical, please seriously consider a
good therapist. Shop around, and find a good
one, but please go. Don't sit around trying to
hold a gaping wound together with ordinary
band-aids because you are afraid that stitches
will hurt. They probably will, but not as much
as a bleeding hole in your flesh! Look up the
county mental health people in your area. At
the very least, call the Mental Hotline that is
listed in your local phonebook. Asking for pro-
fessional help doesn't mean that you are crazy,
or even that you are mentally unstable. It

means that you are smart and stable enough
to realize that you have a problem, and that
you want to get it fixed.)

OK. Enough lecture. It's question time!
Once again, if you don't remember how to use
the exercises, please go back to Chapter 2 and
re-read them. They are on page 13. Don't do
any that are really too hard for you; but don't
avoid any merely because they are uncomfortable or make you think harder than you feel
like thinking, or because you suspect you
won't like the answers. Trust your instincts and
your mental blocks.

1. Helping others means...

*This is mostly to make sure that you read
the chapter. But, as always, your definition
may not be the same as mine. If it isn't, explain
the differences, and why you feel that way. Just
be honest and fair. The real point is to know
how you define help, and why you define it that
way. As long as you can train yourself to have
your mind with you at all times, you will at least
be making your moral and ethical decisions as
informed, honest choices. The thing to avoid
here is drifting aimlessly, or just having reflexive
answers to all the ethical questions you
encounter. Remember, every single situation is
a special case, and should be treated as such. I
know that is harder; but if you aren't willing to*

do that, you may as well be on one of the paths that deals only with codes and obedience. Even if what you have decided to do is make your own code so that you won't have to think all the time, inflexibility is inflexibility.

2. Accepting help from others means...

Just like the question above, but from the other end of the stick.

3. I feel that I should help someone most when...

Here we begin with the diagnostics. This question will point out two things. One is what you feel is your own strong point; you are much more likely to want to help someone if you are sure that you will be able to do a good job. The other is how much you really want to help people, or how much you think your help is worth. I know that sounds a bit strange, but listen. If the thing you picked was helping people make garnishes for formal dinners, unless you work for a catering service or your social group throws an awful lot of parties there really isn't going to be much call for your help, is there? You might be able to make garnishes like a pro, but you either don't feel that your help in more ordinary tasks is worth very much, or you really would rather not help people at all. A little honesty with yourself will quickly point out which it is. This is also a very physical, almost superficial thing, and might imply that you are more comfortable helping people with tasks than with feelings.

On the other hand, if you responded that you feel you should help when you see people crying, not only are you likely to be helping people quite a bit, but you probably feel competent to help with quite a few different kinds of problems, both physical and emotional.

Be honest, be fair, be loving, and please, please be non-judgmental. These exercises aren't to make you feel like a real slob. Their purpose is to help you understand where you are now. Once you know that in honesty, you can make valid decisions about where you want to go from here. You are bound to go somewhere; life is made up of constant change.

4. I am most likely to ask for help when...

This will diagnose two things as well. One is what you feel the least competent to do, the other is what sort of help you are the most comfortable taking.

5. I should offer to help if...

This little diagnostic question will help you to understand what sort of training and inclination you have. Note that the question doesn't

ask when you do offer help, but when you should.

Lots of us were raised to believe that we should do things that we are actually acutely uncomfortable about doing. When we see ourselves falling short of what we think we should do, we tend to feel pretty down on ourselves.

Make sure that what you think you should do is what *you* think you should do; not what your parents, your friends, or even I think you should do. (I know this whole book is filled to the brim with things I think you should do, but that is because it's me writing it. As I have mentioned before, I don't have all the answers; just some of them that work for me. If your answers fit you better, then use them. All I really ask of you is that you examine your answers honestly.

6. If someone refuses my help, I...

This is to find out what your normal reaction to someone refusing your help is. If you know what you usually feel, then you are prepared when someone refuses your help and you feel your normal feeling. You will know that is just your customary reaction to the refusal, and not necessarily your reaction to this particular refusal. Contrariwise, if your reaction to this particular refusal is different from your usual reaction, you will be able to notice that, and perhaps to figure out why it's different.

Once again, be honest, be specific, and be non-judgmental.

7. I am most likely to refuse to help, even if someone asks, when...

This is a lot like question 3 above, but from another direction. This will let you know where you feel the most vulnerable and least competent yourself. If you are afraid of heights, for instance, you are likely to refuse to help someone string Yule lights from their roof.

I get lost easily, and have a phobia about finding my way around. (This is due to a couple of bad experiences when I was a kid and could barely see. I am quite aware of that. I still hate to be told things like "It's just down this road. You can't miss it." Of course I can miss it. When you are frightened enough, you can miss amazingly obvious things. I am working on this, but I am nowhere near there yet.) I make jokes about my most incompatible sign being "Detour ahead." When someone asks me for directions I virtually always refuse to help. I also explain that if I give someone directions, they would be well advised not to follow them.

You can also learn a lot about yourself by discovering if the thing you are least likely to help with is physical or non-physical in nature, and how common it is.

Just because it's common doesn't necessarily mean you are unwilling to help people.

In my case, for instance, people ask me for directions all the time; but the depth of my fear counteracts the frequency of the request.

Do you see how this works?

Also, if you are being honestly honest with yourself, you know if you enjoy helping people or not.

8. I am most likely to refuse the help of others when…

This is the opposite of the question above. It may point out something that you feel so capable about that you know that you can do a better job with than anyone else. Or it may point out something you are so shy about that you cannot bear the thought of someone else looking at it, even to help. Once again, the point is to make you think; to make you aware of your own feelings of competence, helplessness, or vulnerability.

You will also realize as you answer this question whether you like to be helped or not. You may want to write that down, as well. And then go on to explore why you do or don't. Don't be limited to my questions any more than you are limited to my answers.

9. Offer your help to someone. Pick someone you think will be likely to take you up on it. If they refuse, offer to help someone else. Keep going until someone

accepts. When they do, be "good help." Write down who you asked, what they needed, what you did, and how you felt about it.

This is practice helping for those who don't often offer to help, don't feel competent to help, don't enjoy helping, or are prone not to be "good help." For the purposes of this exercise, please do it my way, even if you disagree with what I think is "good help." Look on it as an experiment. Decide if the reactions of the helpee, the people around, and your own self are more or less desirable than the reactions you usually get when you help.

Go into some detail about what you did, how the person you were helping reacted, how you felt both about your work and the reaction.

A small caveat here. Sometimes, the help you give is perfectly good, and the person you are helping is simply rude or thoughtless.

I recall once when a whole bunch of us spent a great deal of time at a gathering putting a maze together. We were, all of us, willing, capable, and cheerful. We did exactly what we were asked to do, followed directions without argument, and stayed for several hours longer than we had originally agreed to. All of us. None of use were even thanked.

There was nothing wrong with the work we did, or the help we gave; it was the person we were helping who forgot his ethics. At the end,

we all felt used. Some of us regretted working so hard for this particular guy. But we were all glad the maze was up; and we all knew we had done well.

So don't let a bad reaction give you the feeling the whole experiment is a failure. Please try again, with someone else.

10. **Ask someone else for help. Pick someone you think will be able to give it. If they can't, ask someone else. Keep going until someone accepts. Write down who helped you, what you asked for, what they did, and how you felt about it.**

The inverse of the question above. This is primarily for those who have difficulty accepting help. As above, look at it as an experiment.* Don't forget to thank the person who helped you. And when you are doing the "write up" later, be honest with yourself. If you think my methods stink, you should also think about why you think that. Don't let one bad experience ruin the whole thing. And don't go asking for help in the area that you are likely to refuse help in. What would you be trying to prove if you did that?

Be honest, and gentle, and full of love.

---

*Be sure to pick someone who knows something about the area you want help with. Asking a technophobe to help you install your new hard drive is just asking for stress for both of you.

Chapter 6 - Harm

Eight words the Wiccan rede fulfill,
An it harm none, do as ye will.
   –Traditional

An it harm none.*

As long as you harm no one, you are free to follow your own will.

But what does that mean, "Harm no one?"

The dictionary defines "Harm" as "hurt; injure; damage, physical or moral."

I define "harm" as interfering with another's free will; lessening someone's free-dom of choice; causing unnecessary injury; damaging someone, physically, mentally or spiritually; or wantonly destroying something.

And don't forget, when you are trying to figure out if an action you are contemplating will cause harm, that you are exactly as impor-tant as any one else. In other words, don't harm yourself, either!

So what sorts of actions cause harm, by my definition?

---

*As you probably know, "an" in this archaic usage, means "as long as."

Forcing someone to take a certain path, whether by mayhem, manipulation, or magic.

Think about it, dear friend.

Any time that you count your will more important than the will of another, you are harming them.

Whenever you decide that what you want is what you will get, no matter what, you are harming someone.

Whenever you go off half-cocked, and hit someone with your fists, your car, or your words without thought, without love, without regard for what it may do to them, you are harming someone.

Whenever you thoughtlessly go your own way and never notice those around you, there is a good chance that you will harm someone before the sun sets.

And whenever you harm someone, three times the harm will return to you; whether you meant to harm them or not, whether you knew you harmed them or not, whether you believe in all of this stuff or not.

Sometimes it's easy to tell that you are going to harm someone.

Sometimes you have to think long and hard to figure it out.

That's why you must have your mind with you at all times.

You have to think at all times.

And you have to review all the facts honestly, with love.

I began to write this book because I got a phone call from someone who wanted me to do a Tarot reading to tell him if he should perform a spell. This was during the Yule season, and I was much too tired (what with all the parties and stuff) to do any sort of reading; but I told him that I would be happy to advise him if I could, and asked what sort of spell it was.

It was a spell, he told me, to cause a specific person to fall in love with him.

No, I told him. Without doing any sort of reading, without knowing him or his situation, without knowing the person he had in mind, or their situation, or anything more at all. No.

I think it is never ethical to cause a particular person to fall in love with you.

Never.

Not under any circumstances.

It alarmed me that he even had to ask the question.

You see, when you force a person to fall in love with you by means of magic, you are causing all kinds of harm.

You are harming the person you wish to love you, because you are limiting their freedom of choice; you are forcing them down a path that they may never have been meant to take, or one that they should no longer be on.

You are harming them because you are limiting their growth; something that is against all the principals of love that we discussed in Chapter 4.

You are harming the person that they may have been meant to love, because they will not be there when that person needs them.

You are harming yourself, because you are acting from purely selfish motives, (examine them honestly; remember that you have no right or even ability to know what is best for someone else,) with such a low self image that you must seriously believe you cannot obtain love any other way.

You are harming all of your families, and untold other people who come into contact with all of you.

And besides all this, I have never, ever seen it work.

At some level, you know perfectly well that it is wrong. (Once again, be honestly honest with yourself.) And all the grief that you have caused the object of your desire (if you were really thinking of them as a person, you would not do such a thing to them) will rebound on you. It won't be long before you wish with all your heart that you had never done any such thing.

Would you expect a relationship to work if you blackmailed someone into it? No? There is no difference between what is ethical to do by "mundane" means, and what is ethical to do by magical means. So why do you expect a good relationship from a coercive charm?

But what about all the love spells, then?

Are you fated to wander lonely through life, with no love, and no recourse to gaining any through magic?

No, not at all.

I have done love spells.

But the sort of love spell that is ethical to do is one that you do on *yourself;* or for a friend that has asked for help. It is a spell to make you *ready* for love. A spell to enable you to recognize love when it comes along. A spell to make you brave enough to take the risks necessary to begin a relationship. A spell to improve timing; so that you will be at the right place at the right time to encounter love. A spell to draw a particular kind of person, not a particular individual, to you. A spell to let the Lady know that you think you are ready for love. You get the idea. It's the difference between fixing yourself up and putting an ad in the personal section of the paper, and choosing someone you find attractive and putting a gun to their head.

If you really want the love of a particular individual, you should try asking them out! There is nothing unethical about using normal means to try to win the love of any unattached individual! Just don't try to force love by using magic, mayhem, or manipulation. Don't violate her (or his) freedom.

Any time that you force anyone else to do anything, no matter what method you use, you are harming them.

If you honestly think that someone would be better off if she wasn't hooked up with that jerk she is living with, and you tell her so, you are offering advice and trying to help her. (Be careful, though. She may still resent your advice.)

If you tell her that you won't speak to her any more unless she loses the guy, you are attempting to manipulate her; attempting to force her to change for *your* reasons. If she does change, this keeps her from learning her own lessons, and stunts her growth. I think this is wrong.

If you tell the guy that your friend really hates him, and is just waiting for an opportunity to tell him so, you are lying, which is dishonest and harms you; and trying to manipulate the situation, which harms both your friend and her significant other. I think this is wrong.

If you go over there with your boyfriend, and the two of you beat the fellow up until he promises to leave, this is also wrong.

You probably agree that the last is wrong without even having to think about it. But, my dear, the first two are just as wrong, even if they aren't actionable.

Whenever any sort of pressure is used, it is a violation of free will. I think any violation of free will is wrong.

I have a friend who was living with a man that was obviously nothing but trouble for her.

He couldn't keep a job, spent all the money she could earn, and constantly ordered her around. Besides this, he decided to take one of her other friends as a lover, and practically moved the woman into the house right under my friend's nose. She was supposed to be "evolved" and put up with this. (More about that on the chapter about Sex, coming up next.)

All through the several years that the two of them were together, I told her frequently that she would be much better off without him. But that is all I did. I just told her. And I listened to the latest outrage, and did nothing except give advice.

She felt that she needed to find out why she had a long history of picking men that used her; and was sure that if she left this one, she would just find another exactly like him – or even worse.

In the end, she left him when she thought the time was right. And if her life so far since is any indication, she knew what she was doing.

If I had forced her to leave earlier, by may-hem, manipulation or magic, that would have been wrong. There was another man, just like the one she was with, waiting on her doorstep within three days. If she hadn't realized that she picked users, and why, she would have moved in with him because it would have been easier than starting out on her own with

nothing. And she would have been right back in the same situation. Only the names would have changed.

Instead, when she was ready, she moved out and took advantage of my long term offer to move into our basement for a few weeks. From there she moved into the basement of another family who had more room, and finally found a place she could afford to rent by herself. Now she is living quite happily alone there, and has a better job and more money than she has had since I've known her.

You must not pick someone else's path for them, even out of love.

You have no way of knowing what the Gods and that person's Higher Self have planned for them.

Finding out what the Gods and your own Higher Self have planned for *you* is hard enough!

Don't let your appetites control your mind. Appetites are good, and let you know when something is lacking in your life. Without them, it would be easy to neglect our own bodies, and that would be harming ourselves. Just don't let them call the shots without any thought, or you will find that your inner child has become spoiled and petulant.

Any time that you want something, just because you want it, you should check to find out if your getting it will harm someone else.

If it won't, by all means go ahead and do it! We are not a religion that glories in the mortification of the body. Just be very sure that it won't. And look beyond the first effect, like looking beyond the next move on a chess board.

If it's raining out, and you want to go out and splash in the puddles, look at the possible consequences, the ripples if you will, of your action.

You will get wet, muddy feet, and possibly ruin your shoes. You may catch a cold, if you have been exposed to one. (Having cold, wet feet really does seem to lower resistance; I don't know why.) People might see you, and decide you are a lunatic. Children might see you, and decide it's OK for them to splash in puddles if it's OK for a grownup to splash in puddles. You might get hit by a car, if you are splashing in the middle of the street.

Then go back, and examine possible reactions to the ripples.

They are your shoes, and you can afford to replace them if you ruin them. Or maybe you will simply go barefoot. The pleasure of splashing in the water will offset the misery of getting a cold; and anyway you don't think you have been exposed. Due to past actions, the folks on your block decided long ago that you are a lunatic, but harmless. One more silly thing will probably not even be noticed. If you see any children mimicking you, you will tell them to get their parent's permission before they continue. You can even explain that you have your mother's permission. (Don't forget to ask Her!) And you will watch for traffic. So it's OK. No one will be harmed. Go ahead and do it!

Or maybe, when you are going through the list, you realize that they are really counting on you to do a big presentation at work next week, and if you have a cold you will be letting a whole lot of people down. That counts as harm. Better not do it.

Do you see?

The key is to *think;* to consider honestly and lovingly, and then to act consciously with full knowledge and forethought. Don't worry about this interfering with your spontaneity. How long would it take to notice the rain, think through the possible consequences, and be out there with your jean's legs rolled up?

Once you get used to considering all the possibilities, to being aware, to following cause and effect, and being honest and loving, it hardly takes any time at all.

Just remember the ripples.

Be aware that in this society, most of us are surrounded by other folks all of the time.

Another example.

Don't honk your horn to summon the other members of your car pool. Even if you think it is plenty late for everyone in the world to be awake, you have no way of knowing

which of those other houses has the woman who has been up all night with a sick infant and only got the baby to settle down less than an hour ago. Now they are both awake again. You don't know which of those houses is home to the man who works the late shift. He has been in bed just four hours; it's the middle of his night. Which apartment has the child who is dying of cancer. Every moment she can sleep is precious; and now it will be hours before she can sleep again.

Be thoughtful and loving. Park your car, walk to your friend's door, and ring the bell. It isn't your job to be alarm clock for the world!

I think it is wrong to lessen someone's freedom of choice. That is why it is wrong to take something from someone else.

If you steal someone's property, that lessens their freedom of choice. How can they choose to use something that they no longer have, because you have taken it?

This is not the same as not giving them something they ask for. We are under no obligation to expand someone's freedom of choice at the cost of our own. Remember that you are exactly as important as any one else. If someone asks to borrow your bike, and you need it yourself that day, it is not the least bit unethical to tell them no.

If you need to borrow someone else's bike, it is not the least bit unethical to ask to borrow

it. This does not limit their freedom of choice; they can also choose to say no.

But if you find a bike unlocked at the corner when you are terribly late and really need it, it is not ethical to "borrow" it without asking, even if you know who it belongs to, and intend to bring it right back. That means that they will not have it to use; and their need may be even greater than yours. Even if it isn't, this is their bike, and what happens to it should be their choice. Don't limit their choices.

Do you understand?

We don't have to follow small laws, and codes. Our Gods don't stand over us, saying "Don't steal." We don't have rules, because we don't need them. We understand why stealing is wrong; we avoid it because we love others, and seek never to harm them. Because we know that they are just as real, and just as important as we are. We don't need to be threatened with a hell full of fire and brimstone to keep us from injuring one another. We know that the three-fold law is in effect. And besides, we try never to harm others anyway.

My kids are young, so I have a list of rules that I made up. They are expected to follow the rules, and there are set punishments for breaking them. It is a code, just as rigid as the code of any organized religion. But I have told them that the rules are only temporary things, to be used until they understand the reasons for the rules. At that point, the rules will no

longer apply. They will still find themselves doing (or not doing) most of the same stuff; but their reasons will be different.

In just the same way, most of the things in the laws of most of the organized religions were to keep people from doing harm to themselves or others. There is nothing bad about the rules, in themselves. We will often find ourselves doing much the same things. Only our reasons are different. We are not doing them to be obedient children of God, because we are not children, and our Gods expect us to grow up. We are doing the same things, but out of love.

When we ignore what we know to be right, we can't make things OK by asking God to forgive us. We have to go to the person we have wronged, and ask them what we can do to make it right. This is much harder; but I never said this was the easy path.

The next part of my personal definition of harm is to cause someone unnecessary injury. I define injury as something that causes pain, whether physical or emotional.

But "unnecessary" injury? Does that imply that injury is sometimes necessary? Of course it is. The key is to balance injury against injury, and look at the situation honestly and lovingly. (Where have you heard that before?)

If your appendix is rupturing, the surgeon will cause you quite a bit of pain and injury, to save your life.

If your marriage is intolerable, the amount of pain and injury caused to your family by ending it may be considerably less than the pain to all parties caused by continuing in an untenable situation.

Sometimes, a friend might ask you for help that will cause them quite a bit of pain.

For example, suppose you have a friend who has asked you what she can do to get a job. Looking at the situation honestly and lovingly, you realize that the only reason that she doesn't have a job right now is that she lost the last three jobs she had because she doesn't wear the right kind of clothing, she isn't clean enough, and she is consistently late for work in the morning.

You have a choice here.

You can tell her that you cannot help her, thus avoiding hurting her feelings and also avoiding any help you might give her.

You can tell her that the problem is that the jobs she keeps trying to get aren't the sort of jobs you think she would thrive in, and that she should try to get a job working with her hands outside. This might alleviate the problems with her appearance and cleanliness; after all jeans, which are her preferred form of dress, are perfectly acceptable in gardening, and in that sort of job you are expected to get a bit dirty.

You might gently approach the difference in her appearance and habits with what is expected in her chosen workplace.

Or you might try a combination of the two above approaches. A sort of "Well, Sally, do you really enjoy being a receptionist? Or do you think it might be time to consider changing jobs? You really do a great job in the garden; you might be happier as a gardener."

But no matter what she decides, the point will come when you will need to work around to her understanding that part of the reason that she has been unable to hold a job might be because of her problems getting there on time.

Try to minimize the pain; but there is no way to completely alleviate it. It's going to be hard to face the fact that her failure is her own responsibility; that her inability either to go to bed when she knows she should or get up sufficiently early in the morning is causing a direct effect on her job, and how her bosses view her.

If she has a genuine organic problem, and cannot force herself to change her scheduling around so that she can work in the mornings, she might have to take an evening job, no matter what that does to her social life.

You see the problems here, don't you?

Telling her that she needs to bathe more often, wear some decent clothes, and get her backside out of the bed in time to get to work is going to cause her pain, no matter how you couch it.

But letting her think that it is a problem over which she has no control, and allowing her to flounder on losing one job after another, and finally ending up destitute when she asked for your help may cause more.

Do you understand?

You have to balance possible pain against possible pain, harm against harm, injury against injury, and take the one that will cause the least.

Does this mean that the three-fold law is in abeyance as long as you are doing something that will cause growth or healing in the long run?

Of course not.

When you begin to be honest with your friends, and tell them what you perceive to be their problems, rest assured that you will get three times as much of that back, as well!

That is part of the reason that you should wait until asked before you offer your advice - no one appreciates unsolicited character appraisals! And also part of the reason why you should be as gentle as possible even when asked. The main reason, of course, is that you are being honest, loving, and non-judgmental here. Don't assume that clean is "good," or sleeping late is "bad," just because that is the way you happen to feel about your own behavior. Different people have different standards, as well as different attitudes and beliefs. Make sure it really is affecting her job before you tell her that it is.

There is one other type of instance where it is sometimes necessary to butt in and harm someone, without even being asked.

That is when you see someone harming another.

Remember the example about the man who was beating his children in Chapter 2?

Whether you decide to go to the authorities about it or not, I think that you are entirely justified in interceding if you are there and he begins to beat one of them in front of you.

You might choose to do this by saying something, by stepping between him and the child, by snatching the child out of harm's way, or by physically overpowering him. Once again, use the gentlest method that you think will work. But I think you are well within ethical guidelines to let him know directly that you do not approve of his actions, and will not allow him to continue in your presence.

In just such a way, don't wait until someone asks for help if they are the victim of a crime, or if their life is in danger. Go ahead and intervene, and then apologize if it turns out to be necessary. Realize that in order to do this, you may very well end up harming the perpetrator or yourself; but some risks are justified. Be willing to take the "three times," and act with decision.

Think, honestly and lovingly, about each and every action before you act, and you will seldom go wrong.

I, personally, don't think that it is ethical to use magic in such a situation, unless there is no other way to save someone's life. It seems an unfair advantage to me, sort of like looking at the top of the puzzle box when assembling a jigsaw. It also seems to have more ripples and reactions than working "normally" in the "normal" universe. In fact, I am so careful with any magical working, that I customarily insert the phrase, "For the good of all, and by the free will of all," just before the "so mote it be."

The next part of my definition concerns damaging someone. When someone is damaged, they suffer permanent harm. To take someone's bike harms them. To take their leg damages them.

Most of us know not to damage someone physically. That has usually been drummed into us since we were littles, and is easy to spot. We are generally not prone to running around with guns and knives, and we don't get kicks from dismembering others. We tend to realize that our right to swing our fists stops at the beginning of the other fellow's nose.

Much more subtle is the tendency to damage others mentally or spiritually.

Don't think it cannot be done.

Just as you can cause permanent damage to someone's leg, you can cause permanent

damage to someone's mind or spirit. In the case of the leg, it will eventually stop bleeding; rehabilitation will enable the patient to compensate for the loss; and prosthetic legs can be obtained. Mobility can be regained, and it is possible that the person could even pass for someone with two whole legs. They may eventually even be grateful for the experience, which may open doors in education or training not available for those not handicapped. At the very least, they may get a handicapped parking tag out of it.

But they will never be the same.

Nothing will really replace the lost leg.

They will miss it, every day, for the rest of their lives.

So someone can heal from wounds of the spirit. They will eventually stop bleeding. They can find behaviors to compensate for the scars. They may even realize at some point that they have learned valuable lessons that they would not otherwise have had a chance to experience.

But they will never be the same.

Nothing will ever really replace the part of their mind or spirit that has been injured or scarred.

At some level, they will have a sore spot, every day, for the rest of their lives.

That is why it is terribly important what we say to each other, how we treat each other, how we see each other.

We must look at one another in love, honestly and non-judgementally.

A word at the wrong time or place can cause damage.

A broken promise, a thoughtless act, a selfish whim; and someone can suffer for the rest of this life, or longer.

Breaking your promise to someone may cause untold damage. Perhaps they were wounded here before, and have only just begun to trust again. Maybe you were the first person they believed when a promise was made.

Maybe you were the last.

If you cannot avoid breaking a promise, let them know as soon as you can. Apologize. Don't let them think you take your promise lightly, or don't care that you had to break it. Explain the causes and your regret; and ask if there is anything you can do to make it up to them.

Rape is a symptom of the same disease. It creates horrible mental and spiritual damage; and there are more types of rape than physical, sexual rape. Any violent activity that disregards the value of the other person is a form of rape. Even violent verbal abuse can leave a person feeling shaken, violated, damaged.

We all know children who were badly damaged by their parents. You may be one yourself. Most of the parents were not trying to damage their offspring. Some were trying to

prepare the child for "the harsh realities of life" in the only way they knew how.

Some of them simply did not see the kid as a separate individual, different and apart from themselves. To the parent, the child was not real. There was no reason to take it into account. Sexual abuse was no different than masturbation. Hitting the kid because it was in the way was just the same as moving their own arm or leg. There was no realization that this was a person, separate and whole within themselves; someone who could be damaged.

If your child is an extension of yourself, and you feel no pain when you hit them, then there is no pain.

The only problem is that the child is not an extension, and there is plenty of pain, and a good deal of damage.

If you were one of these children, then you must not see your own children the same way. And you must not think that you deserved the pain. Your parent was probably treated the same way by her parent, and knew nothing else. You can go back, and re-parent yourself; find your inner child and give it the love you never got. In this way you can heal the wounds, and the damage will be lessened.

Do not brood on the past, build on it. We all have to, anyway; do it consciously! Learn from your mistakes, and those of others, so that the most possible good may come even from bad situations. It is foolish to make the same mistake twice. But live in the present; this is all we have to mold and mend with.

We must not try to exact retribution ourselves for something someone else has done to us. We cannot know enough about the situation to do this fairly. Instead, we should let the three-fold law take care of it.

Do you understand?

Harming someone will inevitably cause you harm. This is why we don't even harm those who obviously seem to deserve it. We don't know enough about the entire situation to make that kind of judgement call. Picture a great tapestry, with the pattern of all our lives on it. We are each following our own thread, so our noses are right up against the cloth. How much of the pattern can we see?

This doesn't mean that we have to stand there and take it; to turn the other cheek, as it were. We can always vote with our feet. If we don't like the way someone treats us, we can and probably should avoid them.

And we can certainly protect ourselves, if we can't simply leave.

I think that using magic to prevent a certain individual from harming us, or someone who has asked for our help, is ethical. This sort of spell does not interfere with free will, or freedom of choice; it acts on *us*, as protection. It's the difference between using a weapon, and using armor. (In this vein, by the way, I have found that the magic chants used

by children are wonderfully effective. One of the best protection spells we ever did was simply "I'm rubber, you're glue. Your bad stuff will bounce off me and stick to you.")

You can also ask the Gods to make the three-fold law operate swiftly for her, so that she can not help but see the connection. If you do this, however, be very sure that you are doing it with love, not to be vindictive. Remember, it will also cause the three-fold law to operate even more quickly for you!

On rare occasions, one of us may choose to sacrifice our own happiness to stop someone else. This is done because we think the harm that individual is doing is far beyond anything we can tolerate. It is done deliberately, knowing full well that we will suffer three times whatever damage we do. I have never encountered a situation where I thought that was necessary. But the whole point of having ethics, not rules, is to enable us to be able to "throw ourselves on the live grenade" if it ever becomes necessary. We have choices, which we are responsible for. We have minds to think with, and will grow into wisdom.

I only ask you to think honestly, with love, before you take any action. And if you think drastic action is called for, please discuss it with those you trust and respect, and with the Gods.

The last part of my definition concerns wanton destruction. Destruction, in my opinion, causes harm to the Universe. Any time that you destroy something for pleasure, in anger, or simply out of boredom, you are joining the side of the despoilers. You are counting the work of someone else as worthless; as something that matters so little that it is of no account if it ceases to exist. This is especially true if what you are destroying is the work of the Gods; that is Nature. Please, dear friend, think. We are meant to be co-creators with the Gods, forming things of strength and beauty. If you take the opposite tack, and tear things up just to hear the ripping sound, what does that make you?

I am not talking, of course, of the controlled destruction that is necessary to make something new; destruction to get the component parts of something to create something different. That sort of destruction is often a necessary part of the path to renewal, which is why traditionally the Pagan Gods of Destruction are Gods of Rebirth, as well.

When I paint a picture, it involves the destruction of a tree to make the paper, destruction of various earths and synthetics to make the paint and gesso, a certain amount of destruction of my own mucus membranes to get the painting done, because I was sloppy for too many years, and now I pay the price with allergies. All of this is destruction to allow construction. With these destructions I paint a pic-

ture which, I am told, brings beauty and inspiration to many.

Occasionally, things must be destroyed because of the harm or potential harm they may cause. You don't want to leave a dead or dying tree where it is likely to fall on your roof. A freezer that no longer works and is not going to be repaired must have the latch destroyed or removed before it is disposed of. These sorts of destruction actually further creation. Death is part of life.

The kind of destruction I think should be stopped is mindless destruction. It is picking the bark off of trees because you don't have anything else to do just then. (Did you know that this behavior can easily kill a small tree? Should a live thing die to satisfy your boredom?) I am talking about breaking someone's flower beds down because you don't want to walk the four extra feet to the sidewalk. About cutting a hole in the leg of your jeans because there is a pair of scissors on your desk. About tearing all the little tabs with someone's phone number on them off the flyer while you wait for the rest of your group to join you, and letting them fall to the floor. About any wanton, senseless act that destroys something someone else created, just because you have nothing better to do with yourself.

Of course, I am also talking about the large destructive things, like arson or vandalism or oil spills. But which of these types of destruction are you most likely to fall into?

Please, dear friend. Be a creator, not a destroyer. When you create something, even something as simple as a meal, you are a force of life and joy, working for the increase of the universe, for the pleasure of the Gods.

When you destroy for the sake of destruction, even a small thing destroyed without thinking, you are aiding the forces of death and darkness, working for the decrease of the universe, working against the Gods. And I don't mean actual death or darkness here. Those are both part of the cycle. We cannot have life without death, and light with no darkness would be a wearing thing indeed. I am talking about ultimate death and darkness. Non-existence. The cessation of all energy. The end of the cycle.

Please, dear friend, don't work on the side of entropy.

OK. Now for the exercises. Once again, remember to follow my guidelines, found on page 13. And if you feel that any are too hard, or cut too close to the quick, postpone them, or change them so that you can deal with them.

1. Define Harm.

This is to get your definition. Remember, you are not the same person that I am, and your answers will not always be the same answers as mine. You need to work with yours.

2. In what circumstances are you most tempted to harm someone else?

This is to diagnose your own weak point. Be honest, and non-judgmental. If you know that you are most likely to harm someone else when you are tired, or menstruating, for example, you will know to be extra careful during those times. If, on the other hand, you answer this with something like "When I see someone harming someone else." you will need to explore that, and determine why, and what other strategy might work that would not involve harming anyone. Or perhaps this is the sort of harm you are willing to pay the price for.

3. In what circumstances are you most tempted to harm yourself?

Very like the question above, but this will pinpoint your self-destructive times. If the answer is "Right after I break up with some-one," for example, you should try to discover why you become suicidal instead of homicidal. If your answer is "When I get on the scale," you might want to explore your attitude about

*weight; which of society's prejudices you are
buying into here, and why. You get the idea.*

4. **Describe a situation in which it might be
   necessary to choose the lesser of two
   harms.**

   *This is a bit of practice; a simulation, which
   enables you to think out some of your basic
   attitudes before you find yourself in a situation.
   If you actually find yourself in a situation such
   as a mugging, for example, there probably
   won't be much time to do a lot of soul-searching.
   It's helpful to have some of the groundwork
   already laid.*

5. **What would you do in this situation, and
   why?**

   *More practice, just another question to help
   you explore your options and ramifications now,
   when you are safe and can take the time to
   think clearly, without interesting blood chemi-
   cals.*

6. **How much force would you use in this situation, and why?**

   *See the previous two examples, above. If
   you know that you tend to berserk in situations
   where there is danger to yourself or a loved one,
   be honest about that here. Berserking can often*

be avoided by walking away; if that is not possible (it would do no good in a mugging, for example, unless you are the muggee yourself) then use it. Understand yourself, love yourself, don't judge yourself. I know several folk who are alive today because they berserked in a bad situation. I knew several who are dead because they refused to hand over the the two bucks that were in their wallet.

7. Why should you avoid harming someone else, anyway?

This is partly to see if you read the chapter, partly for you to decide for yourself if your ethics should share this with mine. As always, be honest and non-judgmental.

8. Why should you avoid harming yourself?

Once again, partly to see if you read the chapter, partly to explore your own reasons to treat yourself well. This will be hard for some of you; specifically those on the high end of the MegoAntiMego scale, but you need to think about it honestly and carefully. We don't want any knee-jerk reactions here. Please don't merely recite what someone else has told you. Remember, this is not some sort of exam; I will probably never see these pages, they are for you to find out things about yourself.

9. What should you do if you harm someone?

This gives you a chance to do some real soul-searching. If you know that you have harmed someone, whether on purpose or by accident, you should try to review that situation here. After you have honestly thought about what you did, and what you should do to "fix" it, then you should really go out and try doing that thing. If you feel that you can't, try writing me (or your own older self) a letter explaining why you can't. If, as you write the letter, you find that these are excuses, not reasons, then go on out and do it!

10. How might you harm someone through inattentiveness?

This is to get you thinking along these lines. A lot of the harm we do, we do because we are thoughtless, not because we are malicious. We need to be more aware of what we are doing, and of what form the "ripples" of our actions may take. As you may have heard someplace before, you need to have your brain with you at all times.

Please don't use this as a forum for self-abuse. We all make mistakes. I make plenty all the time, try as I may to avoid them. (So many, in fact, that at times I wondered if I was qualified to write this book.) And it seems the more

ethical we become, the more our mistakes bother us. But I think it's better to try to avoid them than to blunder on good-naturedly and leave harm in our wake.

CHAPTER 7 - SEX

Let My Worship be in the heart that rejoices, for behold– all acts of love and pleasure are My rituals.
   –Charge of the Goddess
   If it weren't for sex, I wouldn't even be here!
   –Anonymous

(My husband tells me that I should put a line about violins in here. After all, everyone knows that a book sells better if it contains sex and violins!)

We are a nature religion, and nature glories in sexuality. All those beautiful flowers, all those lovely birdsongs, all the brightly colored butterflies are sexual expressions.

We, also, enjoy sex; just as we enjoy all expressions of joy, love and freedom. Sexual expression is fun! It can be a joyous, loving manifestation of closeness between two mortals. It can be a renewal of the love between the God and the Goddess. It is a normal appetite, and satisfying it can be wonderful. It is the best way yet known to make babies.

Most Wiccan circles celebrate the Great Rite at every Sabbat or Esbat. When the Priest and Priestess hold up the Cup and Athame*, and say, "As the Athame is to the Male, so the Cup is to the Female, and conjoined they bring forth blessedness," this is what they are doing! It is symbolic sexual union. It is a sacrament that shows the essential holiness of sex. It is an acknowledgement that without sex, most of the life on this planet would cease. Without sex, there would be no evolution, no renewal, no life.

We celebrate life, in all its many manifestations.

So we celebrate sex, in all its many permutations.

We believe that as long as you harm no one, your life is your own.

What does that mean in terms of sex?

It means that if you are both (or all) consenting adults**, then you are free to do whatever you all desire.

It means that we are non-judgmental.

It means that we accept different lifestyles; that if you are gay, or bi, or multi, or anything else we love you just the same.

It means that if you are monogamous, and have chosen one partner to mate with exclusively for life, we love you just the same.

It means that if you have chosen not to

---

*The Athame is the sacred black handled knife of the Wiccae. Traditionally, it is double edged and leaf shaped. It is one of the working tools of the craft.

**See next page. The footnote was too long to fit here!

have sex with anyone else at all, we love you just the same.

It means that I will not force my preferences on you. Please don't try to force yours on me!

As with all other aspects of our ethics, this too must be treated with love and honesty, thoughtfully and non-judgementally.

It means harm none.

If you use social pressure to force your girl friend to have sex with you, you are harming her. Even if you don't hold her down by main force and rape her, you are causing her to do something she doesn't want to do. If you use phrases like, "How can I show you how much I love you, if you won't love me physically?" or

---

**Sexual union with sub-adults, even sexually mature ones, is illegal, whether you think it is immoral or not. Violating a statute can harm many, because it gives fuel to the fires of those who seek to say we are Satanic, and should be burned.

We know that we don't have anything at all to do with Satan, and that, as it's said, you have to be a Christian in order to be a Satanist; otherwise you are going to a great deal of trouble to insult a piece of bread!

But some people don't see it that way. For many, we are on a vast battleground, and anyone not with them is against them. They cannot accept the fact that we have nothing to do with Satan, because they are sure that we are really doing his work for him, and he's just deceived us into thinking that we are not. There is no convincing them, because they simply assume that we have no idea what we are talking about. All we can do, now that it's widely known that we are not fictional (and I personally think that blowing our cover like that may have been a great mistake) is to show them through our lives that we are not allied with any power that lies, destroys, or generally acts immorally. Breaking laws does not show that.

Some laws *do* need to be challenged. I feel they should be challenged in court, where they can be changed. If you think a law is unjust consider fighting it, not just breaking it!

"I know our parent's wouldn't have done anything like this, but we are more evolved than
they were." or "Really enlightened people
know that physical love is just a greater
expression of spiritual love, and can never be
wrong." or "How can I teach you if you won't
let me get close to you?" you are attempting to
make her have sex with you, although she
doesn't want to. How is that different from
rape? In my mind, it may be *worse* than rape,
because you are manipulating her into believing that she has no choice but to choose your
path for her; into pretending that she is willing.

Who wants to lessen someone's expression
of love?

Who wants to appear unevolved, or unenlightened?

Who wants to remain in ignorance?

I feel that using levers like these is quite
simply unethical. If you honestly examine your
own motivations, I'll bet you find that you are
just horny. If you look at the person with love,
I'm betting that you discover that you don't
want to force her into anything.

To "show how much" you love someone,
listen to what they say. If they are saying "No,"
then respect their "no."

If "we are more evolved" we should realize
that manipulation is just another method of
forcing; more subtle, perhaps, but no less
harmful than using a gun.

If we are "really enlightened people," we should realize that people must be free to do whatever they think they should do, as long as they harm no one themselves.

And I think that refusing to teach the Craft unless someone allows you to use them is as wrong, and unethical, as it gets.

Listen to me, my friend, because this point cannot be stressed enough.

Traditionally, it has always been considered very wrong to charge anything for instruction in the Craft, because it implied that this knowledge was for those wealthy, and consequently worldly, enough to afford it. It implied that the gifts of the Lady could be purchased. It implied that the teacher was nothing more than a paid hireling.

I, also, think that we should not ask payment for passing on the mysteries of our Craft. Partly because to do so is against the very principals of love and wisdom on which the Craft is founded.

If you love someone, you help them freely.

If you are wise, you know that the more wise people there are, the better off everyone will be.

Partly I think we should not charge because I think that our need to earn money might over-ride our own wisdom in regarding whom to teach.

I have released students because the way they learned best was not the way I teach best,

and I knew of other teachers I thought would be more appropriate for them.

I'm not sure I would have had the courage to do so had they been paying me money I badly needed.

You may disagree. You may decide it is only fair to be paid for your time, in spite of centuries of tradition that say we do not charge.

If so, that is your choice.

But please, do not ever charge sex. Never.

Physical love is a gift from the Gods, and is meant to be given freely.

If it isn't given freely, but forced or coerced, then you are mocking the Gods and their gifts.

The Gods tend to dislike this.

If you think you have wronged someone sexually, be brave. Go to the person you have wronged, apologize, and offer to do whatever you can to make it better. Many of us have survived various forms of sexual abuse; it isn't necessarily fatal either physically, mentally, or spiritually. The Gods can even use it to make us stronger and better people if we let them. But this never means that it is alright to perform it.

And lest you get the idea that I think that sexual misconduct is a crime perpetrated exclusively against women by men, let me clear this up now. Anyone can attempt to use anyone. I have known of women forcing, or shaming, men into having sex with them as well; and men telling men that this was what bonding was about; and women pressuring other women to get into bed with them.

Because of the frequent misuse of sex in this culture, many people have confused ideas of when sex is expected.

Some think that any physical affection is a prelude to sex. Some think any nudity implies that sex is bound to follow.

This can cause a great deal of anxiety, confusion, and misunderstanding.

If your group is used to worshipping skyclad,* but one member is very uncomfortable with this, don't just ignore the problem. Discuss it. Help him to discover just what about it bothers him. Does he mind if the rest of you are skyclad as long as he is robed? Be accommodating.

Don't kick someone out or make them feel unwelcome because their standards are not the same as yours, as long as they are not trying to force their standards on you, or ridiculing you for having different standards.

Don't stay with a group that forces you to do something (anything) that you feel is wrong, or that you are uncomfortable with.

Not everyone is comfortable with the idea of sex.

Many people who are uncomfortable have good reason to be.

---

* Nude. Clad only in the sky.

Say that when you were small, your brother held you down one day and force fed you a gallon of pistachio ice cream as a joke. You felt completely helpless while he was doing this, and afterwards you got very, very sick. It's probable that the mere sight of pistachio ice cream now conjures up those same feelings of sick helplessness.

Pistachio is not a common flavor, so you can avoid it most of the time. (You hear about it a great deal more than you are offered it.) When it comes right down to it, you probably don't think about it very much, although ice cream at all makes you a tad queasy.

But say that you begin hanging out with a group of people who eat pistachio ice cream all the time. You really like lots of other things about them, and you can ignore the fact that they enjoy something you would rather not have to think about. You can probably disregard this one aspect of their lives. You can probably even risk seeing a box in the freezer. Unless they offer you some.

If they do, and they allow you to refuse, then all is well.

If they notice that you are uncomfortable when they are eating it in front of you, and stop, then you will probably notice that, and be glad.

If they don't pressure you, you may decide to try it again some time. Or you may not.

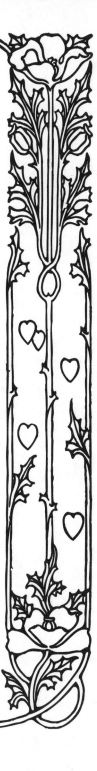

But if they tell you that there is no good reason in the world why you shouldn't like pistachio ice cream, if they insist that you try it, if they needle you and tease you, you will be uncomfortable. You may find it necessary to find other friends.

If they try to force it down your throat, it will be exactly like the last time, and all the feelings and horror will resurface as if it were happening all over again, and you will react as strongly as if they were your brother now, and all the years of suppressed trauma will only exacerbate your reaction. In other words, you are likely to freak. This is natural, and understandable.

You are not at fault here, whatever they may tell you about pistachio being a natural thing and your over reaction being unbecoming. They are the ones who are behaving unethically, for not being loving, honest, and compassionate enough to see that this was a sore spot for you.

Now reread this little story, substituting "sex" for "pistachio ice cream." (Well, alright. I don't know how much a gallon of sex is, either; and I must admit that I don't know anyone who keeps boxes of it in their freezer. Stop being so literal, and look at the meaning of what I am trying to get across.) If you, or someone you know, is uncomfortable with the idea of sex, assume that there is a reason for it.

If you are uncomfortable with sex (or anything else, for that matter,) try gently to explore the reason. Self knowledge is a key step toward honesty and understanding.

If someone else in your group is uncomfortable with the notion, assume that they have good reasons. As we discussed in the chapter about love, don't expect them to want to discuss the reasons with you, either. If they want to, fine; but don't press them. Allow people their privacy. Respect their wisdom about their own lives.

Sexuality is a tender subject. For some, the tenderness is the tenderness of love. For others, it's a bruised and sore spot. Please remember that. Don't behave like some of the folks I've heard of, who assume that someone who doesn't want to have sex must simply be unaware of how wonderful it is; that they would be "cured" if they got some - so here it comes, ready or not. They may be far too familiar with the other side of sex in this culture. With the forced, brutal parody of sex that simply proves that one individual has power over another.

If you try to force them, they will most assuredly not enjoy it or find it wonderful, even if they have never had sex before. If you let them grow naturally, and support them in any decision that harms no one else, then they will develop their own sexuality.

It may not resemble yours at all.

Similarly, don't let anyone force you. Turn
around and walk out if you can. If you can't,
and you are raped, remember that this is not
sex at all; this is someone trying to harm you,
to show his power over you. Acknowledge that
he could overpower your body; but your soul is
your own, and he can not touch that. You did
not make this choice, so whatever your sexual
preferences, this does not reflect on them at
all. Even if your body responds, bodies can be
pretty stupid. All they have are nerves and
reflexes, and if they are stimulated they will
fire. This has nothing to do with your choice or
your responsibility. Don't let anyone tell you
that it does. If this is really a sore spot, think
about getting counseling. Be sure to pick a
good therapist, though. Don't keep going to
one if you don't agree with what he says.
Remember that for many of them, having any
kind of religion at all is a sign of instability; let
alone a minority religion like ours. And
"Magical Thinking" is a form of insanity which
must be cured.

It's the same thing all over again, Gentle
Reader. Treat everyone with love, honesty and
respect. Be non-judgmental. Be caring.

What if you want to make love with your
working partner, but he is married to someone
else, and they have two kids? He is willing. In
fact, he mentioned it first. What do you do
now?

Tell him you want to check with his wife to see if it's OK with her.

If he says that's alright, then really ask her. (If he asks you not to, then he knows that she wouldn't like the concept. Don't do it.)

If she says OK, but she doesn't want to hear about it, then she is not comfortable with the idea, no matter what her mouth says. Assure her in that case that you will leave him alone, and leave him alone.

Some people enjoy "open marriages," some don't.

Don't assume that free love is the only right and natural way, and anything else is repressive, puritanical and bad for everyone.

There are plenty of folks who are monogamous by nature or training. This doesn't mean that they are unevolved, unenlightened, insecure, selfish, immature, or any of the other buzzwords that folks use to shame other folks into doing what they want. Nonjudgemental, remember? It simply means that they enjoy the stability and safety of having only one partner, and expect the same of their mate. And we are not simply talking of emotional safety here. We are also speaking of the risk of disease, in a life-or-death fashion. There is nothing wrong with this. What is the difference between thinking everyone should have multiple partners and thinking that no one should? Making value judgements and decisions for others is making value judgements and decisions for others. If you expect those around you to respect your decision to be bisexual, then respect their decision to be monogamous.

In the case of your teacher, it is not only *his* marriage at risk here. It is also *hers*. And any decision that is made will also affect the children. Do you see how?

Look at it this way.

A marriage is an agreement, a promise between two people. If either one breaks that promise, then the trust which is the glue of the marriage is weakened.

If a man's wife is uncomfortable with his sexual decisions, and he doesn't care enough about her to follow the agreement that they made in the first place, that will erode her trust and faith in him.

Once that trust and faith are gone, the days of the marriage are numbered.

There is abundant evidence that broken marriages are bad for kids. Even if all parties try hard to establish a secure, consistent home (or two of them) there is a certain amount of traveling around, of being shunted from pillar to post, of having to make decisions about which parent to favour, of missing someone dreadfully all of the time, and seeing them just often enough that the kid can't simply grieve and get on with her life. It's hard. I remember one of my stepsons standing on a stump as we were leaving him one day, and crying, "I don't know how much longer I can go on like this!"

He was only ten years old. And both of his homes are loving and secure.

Sometimes, this kind of pain is necessary to forestall even greater pain.

But it is never necessary to put others through something like this just to satisfy your own lust.

Be responsible.

Be honest.

Be loving.

Be careful.

Remember, one of the people you don't want to harm is yourself.

Use suitable protection. Take precautions. Behave responsibly, because like it or not, you are responsible.

If you are HIV positive, make sure that all of your partners know this. If you love them, you must give them this choice to make freely. If you don't love them, you may want to examine your reasons for making love with them in the first place. If all you want is sexual relief, that's what your good right hand is for! (Or your left hand, as the case might be. Although my husband points out that that would be sinister.)

(I, personally, am not convinced that a condom is adequate protection, by the way. We are talking about a virus here, after all. Condoms aren't 100% protection against sperm; and any hole that a sperm can get through, viruses can walk through hundreds

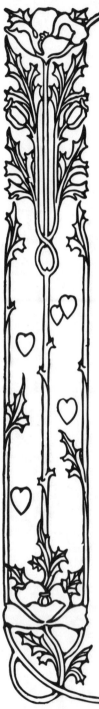

abreast. You might want to take that into consideration when choosing a partner. If you are already HIV positive, you may want to choose your partners from among other folk who are, too. The important thing is that you make the choice consciously, honestly, and lovingly, and that you fully inform your partners before you risk exposing them. Hopefully, a cure will be found soon, and this will not be the life-and-death thing it is now for much longer. But as long as it is, you must be aware, and act with loving consideration.)

Remember, our religion is about freedom, wisdom, love and responsibility.

It is also about joy, laughter, life and growth.

So enjoy sex, however and with whoever you wish, as long as you harm no one!

But what if you have no partner, let alone multiple partners, and no expectations of having any any time soon?

Sex, in this country, is used so much to sell everything from movies to beer to cars that we tend to be inundated with it. This might give you the impression that everyone else is having sex all the time. You might even feel that there is something wrong with you if you haven't had any in a while.

Forget that.

It's all hype.

Long periods of involuntary celibacy are normal.

The birds and the bees themselves go without for months at a time. (Most of the bees, in fact never get any at all!) This is no reflection on you, or on your desirability or lovability. It simply means that you are not in the right place or time for a while.

Even married folk and couples with long term relationships have this problem sometimes. She may be having a difficult pregnancy. His back is bad for a while. She has horrible cramps and headaches when she is menstruating. He has periodic impotence. These things happen. (Although couples can find hundreds of other ways to show their love physically besides sex. Use your imagination!)

Don't despair.

After my first marriage broke up, I was sure that I was doomed to be alone for the rest of my life. I was wrong. Unless you sabotage yourself, you are very likely to find a partner eventually (if you want one.)

I can tell you this, though. If finding someone is the most important thing in your life, you are sabotaging yourself. Not only are you wearing a big sign that says "predator" on your forehead, you are not developing anything to offer a potential mate. No one is interested in a long term relationship with someone who is boring, demanding, clinging, or obsessed with simply having a relationship.

If you are in love with love, you are not seeing anything clearly, and your relationship is not with your partner at all, but with a fantasy. Only if you are in love with your partner can your relationship thrive.

I strongly suggest, by the way, that you not actually marry anyone unless you cannot imagine living without them. Marrying for any other reason will eventually cause trouble. You may be able to work through it, but there will be trouble.

So don't lose heart!

Be joyful, which is extremely attractive!

Remember what I said about love spells in Chapter 6, and go gladly into the world, knowing that the Lord and Lady approve of sex, and that they will see to it that *all* your needs are met, if you let them.

Live, laugh, and love with sex or without it, for the good of all, and by the free will of all.

Exercise time. No; no field exercises I'm afraid. Although if you have a willing partner, feel free to include some. Most of us enjoy sex quite a lot, and we are pretty firm about that! (If we weren't firm, it wouldn't be half the fun! No!! I can't believe I *said* that!) Once again, please follow the guidelines for doing the exercises, as stated in Chapter 2. You will find them on page 13. Don't do any of these if you feel that you can't. This isn't a final, with a due date. Postpone them until you feel comfortable dealing with the subject.

1. My idea of perfect sex would be _

This is to get you started with perfectly safe fantasy things. Fantasies can be enormously satisfying, and they never hurt anyone. They can also tell you a great deal about yourself. After you have finished describing your perfect experience, ask yourself what about it makes it perfect. What is there that you need? What is there that you aren't getting? You can get a great deal of insight from this. You can also share this with your partner, if you wish. Acting out a sexual fantasy can be fun. It can also be disappointing, so be careful here. Some things work better in the abstract than in the concrete.

If you can't stand to think about this entire subject at all, then don't. Skip it! These questions will still be here when you do feel like exploring this area.

2. My sexual bias is _

This is self exploration. If you are in the closet, you can come out to this page, anyway, even if you feel you have to destroy it later. Exploring your feelings, motivations, and perceptions can be enlightening, even if you are already quite clear about your orientation. Are you happy with your feelings? Do you think that you "should" have a different bias? Why? Whose values are you actually using here? Remember that we are all different individuals,

and as such we have individual differences. Don't be a captive of your own prejudices. Remember to be honest, loving, and non-judgmental.

3. My parent's attitude about sex was _

This will give you some idea of why you may have some of the feeling you were dealing with in question 2 above. If you were raised to be tolerant of homosexuals, then you are probably comfortable with yourself if you are one. If you were raised to think of them as sinful or sick, then you will have to deal with some self-doubt, or maybe even self-hatred.

On the other hand, you may have been raised to be strictly monogamous or celibate. If so, you have a whole different can of worms to deal with if you have decided to be sexually active with multiple partners. Or perhaps you were raised with freedom and sexual expression, and now find that you are happier being celibate or monogamous. Do you feel that you are letting someone down somehow? Not doing your duty to your fellow man? As always, be fair and honest. Don't make your parents out to be villains. They were, themselves, raised by their own parents; and the standards then were likely to be stricter than what they taught you. Realize that whatever you were taught, it is only something you were taught as a youngster; not something that is intrinsically true.

4. The part of sex I am most comfortable with is _

This is to find your own starting point. That part that puts you at your ease. If you know where you are most comfortable, then you have something you can initiate if you begin to feel uncomfortable with a developing situation. If you find things moving just a bit too fast, you might want to redirect the activity, rather than curtail it. If you like kissing, for instance, and your partner begins to do something you are uncomfortable with, you can return to kissing. He will probably go along; kissing is fun, too. And then you can kiss for a while until your anxiety has abated, or your excitement has risen, and you are ready to try what he wants to do. If it doesn't, or he is not so easily distracted, it is time to be honest with him and explain that you are not comfortable with what he is doing now. Expect him to accommodate you, as you would not force him to try something he didn't want to do. If he won't, vote with your feet. He seems to be more involved with himself than with you, anyway.

On the other hand, if your favorite part of sex is the chocolate, you may want to avoid sex altogether until you become more comfortable with the basic concept. It is just possible that you are missing the point, here.

5. The part of sex I am least comfortable with is _

This lets you know where you feel the most fragile and vulnerable. Or perhaps simply where something does not feel good at all. I hate pinching, for instance. It doesn't feel nice one little bit to me. I find it painful and annoying, and nothing can get me out of the mood more quickly. My husband likes it. So I pinch him, and he doesn't pinch me. This is because we love each other, and know that we don't have exactly the same tastes, no matter how close we are in many, many ways.

If you know what you don't like, then you can ask your partner to avoid that ahead of time. If he uses this knowledge as a lever against you, it is time to have a serious discussion with him. If he is trying to cause you discomfort or pain, how much can he really love you? If he won't stop, you might want to think about voting with your feet. Get up and walk away a few times, and he may realize that you really mean it. If he won't, perhaps you should walk farther.

6. Sex is wrong when _

Here we go again. Did you read the chapter? Do you agree with me? Do you have other instances which are your own personal examples of just how wrong sex can be? Or do you think it is never wrong? (If you honestly think this, please go back and re-read the chapter. It is easier to damage someone using this lever than any other.) Whatever you think, and whatever your reasons, explore and explain them. This is how you will build your own personal ethical sense.

7. Sex is right when _

More of the same. When do you think sex is appropriate? Where? With whom? Using what? (Didn't expect that one? Maybe you should explore a bit what you think about "toys.") Go into some detail. It is important to concentrate on when it is good to do something, as well as when it is bad; specially if it is something you are not terribly comfortable with in the first place.

This doesn't mean that you have to run right out and have sex if you don't want to. Remember that you shouldn't do anything you are uncomfortable about doing. If you are uncomfortable, there is a reason for that, too. Find it out, if you can, but don't force yourself.

8. If I have sex with someone, it means _

This is to find out what sex means to you. Does it imply a deep commitment, or is it simply a "you scratch my back, I'll scratch yours" kind of arrangement. It is important to know

what it means to you, because without this knowledge, you are likely to find that you may have thought this was "you scratch my back," but now you find that a little voice inside you is deciding what to name the children and picking out retirement plans.

It is also a good idea to be able to compare meanings with a potential partner. If you mean "it feels great, and shows our friendship" and she means "it's an engagement" someone is about to be terribly hurt. If we are going to go through life harming none, we need to know these things ahead of time.

9. What makes sex a holy act?

This is a religious question. It is here to help those on this path to explore more about the Godheads. If you are not on this path, you may want to simply skip this one. (Or you may not. Perhaps your Gods are party animals, too.) If you want to know more about what, exactly, this path I keep talking about is, I have some stuff about that in the appendix.

10. Who benefits the most from sex?

This explores some of your deepest thoughts and feelings about the entire sexual act. As always, be honest and non-judgmental. You may find your answer to this, or any of the other questions, changing over time. Just write and examine what you think here. Maybe you think your partner gets more out of it. If so, why? Maybe you feel you do. If so, why? Maybe you think the Gods are the ones getting the greatest good from this. Once again, if so, why? Or perhaps you think the ones who get the most from sex are the babies who are being conceived!

CHAPTER 8 - WILL

Make it so.
  –Traditional Sea Captain

Well, now we have most of the parts of the Wiccan Rede together, but what exactly is meant by the phrase "as you will." It's just another way of saying "what you want," isn't it?

No, not exactly.

Will involves a bit more than just wanting.

If you want something, you would like to have it, or like for it to happen. This is a desire; an emotion.

If you *will* something, you focus your desire and make a tool of it so that what you desire will, in fact, come to pass. This is an action. It takes conscious thought, movement of energy, direction. It's not an emotion, and there is nothing vague or fuzzy about it. It can be enormously powerful. That is why it is not something to be taken lightly. You must, as I may have mentioned before, have your brain with you at all times.

It's the difference between sitting in the living room, and thinking that an apple would sure taste good, and getting out of the comfy chair, going into the kitchen, and getting one.

In the military, they never say "You should get up at 0500." They say, "You will get up at 0500." The possibility that you might not never enters the equation.

In just the same way, when we will something, the possibility that it might not happen never enters our minds. If it does, then we are just wanting, not focusing our wills. Magic works because we know it will work. We don't think it will, or hope it will, it simply will. And so it does.

We make it so.

Does this mean that anything we think about will actually happen?

Of course not!

When we are angry, we sometimes find ourselves imagining terrible things happening to the person who is angering us. And of course we get angry too. None of us is perfect. If you never get angry at all, it's probably because you have arranged your life to avoid such encounters.

I had no occasion to get angry for years. I freelance, so I don't have a boss. I seldom drive anywhere, so traffic didn't bother me. The cats were long grown, and trained out of kittenish behavior. My husband is one of the most wonderful men in the world, and we had long since made the compromises necessary to live together. My computer is a Macintosh, and works like a champ. I never watch the news, I don't have time to sit in front of the TV. Nothing bothered me, because there were no irritants; but I thought I had this whole thing licked.

Then my stepsons, aged 12 and 9, moved in. Suddenly, I found that I could still get amazingly angry, if there were reason enough. I'm not even sure that the anger is a bad thing. After all, I'm fighting for their lives here! I firmly believe that if they grow up to be lazy or inconsiderate, if they don't learn to empathize with the other guy, if they aren't honest and thoughtful, if they can't think rationally, then their lives will be much harder. When they are grown, they may choose to live their lives in a completely different manner than that I am now teaching them. But they will be able to make the choice. They will know these skills. Und, they vill *LIKE* dem!

They have been here for a couple of years now, and I have less and less occasion to be angry with them. But I have learned my lesson, anyway. I know that I will always be able to get angry if things matter enough. If I don't get angry, chances are it doesn't really mean much to me.

Even when we do get angry, though, nothing happens unless we will it to happen. There is a difference between fantasizing that the clerk in the store who claims he can't find the mixer you need when you can see it on the

shelf right behind him will trip and fall face
first into the fool box so that his nose breaks
on the call letters, and maybe then he'll notice
them; and pushing him so that he actually
does.

There is a difference between longing that
your boss would just fall down dead, and getting a gun.

There is a difference between wishing for a
thing, and willing it.

Go ahead and fantasize and wish all you
want. But don't put any will behind it.
Thoughts are just thoughts, unless you will
them to be things.

But what is the real difference, you ask.
How can I be sure my thoughts don't become
real? How can I know that the automobile accident my boss was involved in had no connection to my sincerely wishing for him to try to
work when he's in pain?

It's simple, really.

If you don't want any harm to actually happen, and you are afraid that it might if you
concentrate on it, or daydream about it, then
assume while you are daydreaming that this is
only a daydream. Actually repeat it to yourself;
both before and after your vengeful thoughts.
"I know this is just a daydream, but I sure wish
that he could find out how hard it is to concentrate when he's in pain. I just hope that someday he finds out what it's like to have to come
to work when you feel like this. I wish I had

the nerve to just go up to him and punch him really, really hard in the stomach so that he would get an inkling of what I'm going through right now, and lay off me. This is just a fantasy, though, and has nothing to do with the real world." This gives you a vent for your anger and frustration, and harms no one.

When you do decide to will something, however, you need to be clear about what you are going to do, and to proceed honestly and lovingly.

We focus our wills. The very word "focus" means to bring things together until we can see clearly.

This is why it is so important to be able to correlate cause and effect, and to be aware of the ripples that will probably be the result of any action you take.

On this path, we don't wander aimlessly through the world, we walk purposefully, with our eyes wide open.

Think of life as a river. Parts are smooth and broad, parts have rapids, parts are straight and you can see a long way ahead, parts are twisty and your vision is quite limited. Everyone on this river is issued a canoe and a single paddle. How you wield your paddle makes all the difference.

You can try to fight the current, and wear yourself out paddling upstream, only to find yourself being swept along anyway.

You can flail around, with no idea what you are doing, and find that your canoe is spinning in circles, or going sideways part of the time, which can be painful and dangerous.

You can take control, and paddle manfully ahead, expending a great deal of effort to get where you were going anyway.

You can lay back, put your paddle in the canoe with you, look up at the sky, and go wherever the river takes you. If you do, of course, you are likely to wind up on a shoal someplace; but hey, the river's like that.

You can let your paddle trail in the water, lean over the side, and admire your own reflection; but then you have no idea what is coming up and you are likely to get some surprises, and not all pleasant ones.

Or you can learn to use your paddle like a rudder, look as far ahead as you can see, and go at the pace of the river but in your direction. This is my choice. I like to glide effortlessly along, making little noise or disturbance, enjoying the sights, but in control of my own canoe.

That is what using your will is like.

We don't buck the current.

We don't rush to where we are going anyway. We aren't the once-born. We have time.

But we don't simply lie back and let life happen to us, either.

We know what we are doing, and why we are doing it.

If we don't like the direction life is taking
us, we exert just enough subtle pressure to
change the direction. No huge confrontation
with the boss that gets us fired and blacklisted.
Just a quite word in private, a "I'm sorry, Sir. I
probably shouldn't have come in today, but I
need the money. I seem to be coming down
with flu, and have horrible stomach cramps.
Please cut me a bit of slack here, and I
promise I'll make it up as soon as I am able."
Give him a chance to be sympathetic and
understanding. You might be surprised, if you
don't ask too often.

If you are a student of human nature, if
you have learned to correlate cause and effect,
you know that if you question him in public,
he will be forced to take the hardline, and be
tough. Otherwise, he knows that people will
take advantage of him.

If he won't be understanding, and you
can't stand it any longer, you can simply send
out applications to other jobs. It is not ethical
to force him to change, but it is ethical to vote
with your feet.

Similarly, if you are experiencing sexual
harassment, standing up and yelling "Stop sexually harassing me!" will force the guy to be
defensive. He has little choice. He has to deny
that he did it, or claim that you were asking
for it, or he is guilty of a crime and looses lots
of face as well. If, on the other hand, you qui-
etly tell him, "Sid, I don't consider that a com-

pliment, I don't think it's appropriate, and I don't like it. Please stop." he has a chance to apologize and stop. He will probably be sarcastic about it, but that is because you refused something he may have meant as a compliment or a pass. That's an uncomfortable position for him, but it's not untenable. He is likely to stop if that sort of thing is not a deeply ingrained habit, just to avoid the possibility of future embarrassment. If he doesn't, a quiet "Sid, I said stop, and I meant it. Does the word 'lawsuit' mean anything to you?" might turn the trick. If not, that is the time to bring out the big guns. Find out if it's just you, or if he is harassing all the women at the office. If he is, all of you might get together at once and confront him. If he is vastly outnumbered, he may realize this is a real problem that he will not easily get out of.

If he still doesn't stop, that is the time to go to his boss, or start other action.

Treat everyone with honesty and love, remember? Even when they are acting like slime buckets, like Sid.

If it comes to a fight, then be prepared, and fight to win. (If you don't mean to win, why are you fighting?) Be calm and rational if you can, and blazing with anger if you can't. But have your reasons and objections ready.

Fight fair.

We have rules for fair fighting in our house, which *will* be used in all arguments. I've been told I should list them here, so here you are.

ROBIN'S RULES OF FIGHTING

1. Be rational.
2. Stick to the point.
3. If you aren't sure what the point is, ask for clarification or definition.
4. Don't bring up a third party.
5. Don't make personal remarks.
6. If you realize that you were wrong, admit it. Everyone is wrong sometimes.

Even if the person you are fighting with doesn't know or follow the rules, you can. Simply ignore any remarks that aren't pertinent to the fight. Most people can't stand to be ignored, especially during an argument, and will answer your remarks if they can't sidetrack you.

If you have reason on your side, you will probably win at least a moral victory. (If you don't have reason on your side, you should stop fighting as soon as you realize that.) Moral victories are important too; enough of them will change anything.

Just remember, even when you find that you have to fight, to ground your fight in love, not in fear or hatred. Move purposefully and surely to your goal, knowing that you have chosen it wisely, honestly willing to harm none, being non-judgmental and caring about all those you encounter as the real, important people they are. This is the stuff that Witches are made of.

Go softly and joyfully through the world.

Know where you are going, and why.

Be awake and aware.

Do things because you will to do them, not because you just do them.

Keep your brain with you at all times.

But above all, walk with love and laughter in your heart, and you cannot drift far from the path.   .

Alright, exercises again. Remember how to do them? (If you don't, check back to page 13.) As always, skip those that feel too hard, and come back to them another time.

1. What is the difference between wanting something and willing something?

This is to see if you read the chapter, and also to see if your own definition is different than mine. As I have often said before, we are different people; and even if your ideas resemble mine quite a bit, there will be differences. I have shown this manuscript in progress to several people. Every one of them has their own comments about how I could clarify a point, or make another one. This is your chance to do

that. To write your own book on ethics, if you will.

2. How do you tend to handle your canoe on the river of life?

This is self-examination and diagnostics again, and might be really hard. Don't be limited to one of the ways I listed. Think about your life, and the way you live it, and make your own analogy. Maybe you know that you have a tendency to be a meddler, but do nothing about directing your own life. Perhaps then you might draw an analogy that you drift along, trailing your hands in the water to make ripples and stir it up. Do you get the idea, dear friend? This might be a good one for meditation. If you can understand the way you handle your canoe now, you can decide what you want to do with it in the future. As always, be fair, honest, loving, and gentle with yourself.

3. Is this the way you want to handle it? Why or why not?

More information on the same theme. Are you satisfied with the way you are living your life? If you are, list the reasons why you are glad that you are living the way you do. If not, list the reasons why the way you are living now will no longer serve you. Again, use your standards, not mine. Maybe you honestly think that the best way to get ahead is to paddle hard, so that you can cover more of the river before you have to change canoes. (We do believe in reincarnation, here.) If so, say so. Be non-judgmental. Be honest and loving. Be specific. If you are tired of drifting, because you will never have enough money to get a decent car as long as you are stuck in this job, say so. Don't write "My life doesn't seem to be getting anywhere." write, "I am tired of working for $4.00 an hour. At this rate, I will never be able to save a down payment for a car, and I need to be able to buy a reliable car so that I can get away into the mountains when this city life really begins to get to me." It is just possible, if you are specific like this, that you will find that what you really need is not a car, but a move to the mountains! That might not really require more money, after all. If that is your only reason to change the way you want to live your life, perhaps you should change where you live your life, instead. Remember, be non-judgmental. The way I have chosen to live my life may not be the best way to live yours.

4. How can you handle it differently if you want to? Be specific.

Further exploration of the same question. This is the place where you can list specific things you can change to live your life differently. If you like the way you are handling your

canoe now, then skip this question of course. If
not, what can you change to make things different? Remember, be gentle with yourself. And
don't pick enormous, sweeping changes, either.
It's terribly difficult to change like that
overnight. Pick things you can really do. Not,
"I'm tired of drifting; I need to stop drinking,
start college, and get my PhD." Instead, write
"I'm tired of drifting; I need to join AA, and
begin to work on my drinking problem." One
step at a time. (Well, 12 steps in that particular
case, but you get the point, right?) Once again,
be honest, fair, loving, and gentle with yourself.

5. What is going on in your life right now?

This question is to get you to pick your
head up and look down the river, in case you
haven't been paying attention. Even if you really
want to go through life looking at your reflection, please try this exercise. You might be surprised. What you ultimately do with any of the
material in this book is your choice, of course.
But as long as you are still working through it,
you can try it my way this once, can't you? Be
honest and specific again. I know I am saying
that a lot, but remember that I don't know
what order you are doing these exercises in, or
how many weeks it's been since you last looked
at this book. The love and honesty are important, and you should not do any of these exercises without them.

6. My most important goal right now is_

This is to begin goal setting, if you haven't done this before. If you have, this will be easy. If not, it will be harder. But if you have no goals, how can you steer?

To find out what your goals are, begin with something easy, small, and material. "I want the new Gael Baudino book." Then ask yourself why you want the book. "I want to find out what is happening to the Colorado Elves, and how she is going to weave the Wiccae into this." Why again, "I want to know what she has to say about the Craft." Why again, "I want to know as much about the Craft as I possibly can." Why again, "I want to become the best Priestess that I can possibly be."

Keep going until you have dug down to an actual goal. It will be there, even if the path is completely different. Even if it leads through "I want to read it; I want to be doing something other than my day to day stuff; I'm bored with my life; I hate my job; I don't think that what I am doing is helping anyone; I want to make life better for children; I want to own and operate a day-care center."

If your digging leads to something you haven't tried, like the day care, then volunteer with one a bit before you quit your job and try to open one. You might like the idea of working with children, but find that trying to keep 20 of the little creatures from running off in 30 differ-

ent directions and killing each other is more
than you can actually deal with. (Yes, 20 kids
can run off in 30 or even 40 directions. If you
have ever worked with them, you know this.) In
that case, you might want to back up one step.
Perhaps instead of actually working with children, you might want to try designing learning
materials for them. You have an "in" with that
day-care center now; field test your designs
there.

I am not advocating stepping off into the
blue unless there is no other choice. If you are
supposed to do that, things will be arranged so
that there is no other choice. I would never have
become an illustrator full time, if I hadn't married an Army man and quite to my surprise
been told that I could no longer teach school.
(They said I would be transferred in the middle
of the year, and that's too hard on the kids.
They were right, by the way. We were transferred to Okinawa.)

Honesty and thoughtfulness here again, of
course.

7. I will be able to reach it if I _

Here is the time for some concrete planning
on how to reach the goal you found in question
6. Be specific, be honest, take reasonable steps.
Not "I am going to open a day care center." but
"I am going to volunteer to work with children
two afternoons a week." If you like it, then you

can progress to "I am going to find a job at a day care center that will pay enough money for me to live on." Then "I am going to quit my other job, and take the job at Sunshine House." Then, after working there long enough that you know what sorts of things you would need to open a day care center, "I am going to make a list of all the things I need to open my own center." Then, "I am going to arrange for all the things on my list except the financing." Then, "I am going to take the list to the bank and arrange for a loan." And only then, "I am going to open my own day care center."

Do you see, my friend?

Possible steps will get the job done. Showing up at the bank with no business plan, no location, and no prospective clients will get you refused. You don't want that, so don't set yourself up for it!

8. The thing I would most like to change in my life is _

More of the same sort of exercise as the goal planning above, but from a slightly different direction. The steps to arrive at the answer (if you don't already know it) are the same. You may wind up with the same answer, or it may be something entirely different. Either way, go with it. If it's the same, this is obviously something that is bugging you a lot. If it's different, then you have two things you can work on. It's

up to you whether you decide to work on them at the same time, or sequentially. If you decide to do them in sequence, which one should be first? As always, loving, gentle honesty is in order here.

9. I think the best way to do that would be to _

Like question 7, this is one to be taken one step at a time. If your answers to questions 6 and 8 were the same, you can skip this one. If they were different, you will need to repeat the same kind of thinking here. If you don't remember what that was, go back and re-read the explanation for question 7.

10. Think of a simple action. Then list all the possible ripples that action might cause. Look forward in time at least a month.

This is to get you looking at actions and consequences of those actions. Cause and effect sort of stuff. If you are unused to thinking about more than the first ripple of reaction, you should consider doing this more than once, with more than one action. Write down what you think will happen. Then actually try the action, and follow it for as far as you can. Try to find out if your predictions were accurate. If not, try to discover why, and do the exercise again. Keep doing it until you can predict what the outcome of your actions will be with a fair amount of accuracy. None of us (except perhaps the really great precogs) have total accuracy. But you can develop enough working accuracy to steer your boat!

Chapter 9 - Ethics

"What wrong were you doing all day, Curdie? It is better to come to the point, you know," said the old lady, and her voice was gentler even than before.

"I was doing the wrong of never wanting or trying to be better. And now I see that I have been letting things go as they would for a long time. Whatever came into my head I did, and whatever didn't come into my head I didn't do. I never sent anything away, and never looked out for anything to come."

–George MacDonald,
The Princess and Curdie

So now we come to the final chapter of this book.

Here we are going to discuss the whole question of ethics, and try to pull everything you have learned into one big picture.

When you were small, you were taught a certain world view by your parents, your peers, and the people around you. Your mind was primed then, and ready to accept those things that would enable you to adapt in this society. You eagerly learned the concepts that your parents taught you, and by the time you were two, your basic view of the world was in place.

As you grew, you learned to fit the things you heard and saw into that basic view of the world. You learned what behavior was acceptable to the people who ruled your life, and what was not. You learned how much latitude there was in the rules, and when "no" really meant "no."

And you also learned how to work around the rules to get what you thought you really wanted.

If your upbringing had been perfect, you would have perfectly understood the reasoning behind the rules, and you would easily have developed perfect ethics.

The trouble is that we are all raised by mortals; by people who have problems of their own, who were raised by other people with problems and so on. And the problems tend to get passed down from generation to generation, right along with all the other attitudes and beliefs that your parents so carefully instilled in you.

You, however, have decided that at least some of those things are not the things that you want to make up the pieces of your world view. That's great! I think that adults need to create their own world views. We are not the same individuals that our parents are, and we are not living on the same planet they were raised on. The world is changing too quickly.

Population has probably more than doubled since they were young; societal values are shifting; technology has flown far beyond the Science Fiction of my own youth, let alone theirs; incurable diseases have cropped up, and forced a change in attitude about a great many things. Future Shock, they called it twenty years ago. But I look at my own kids now, and they aren't the least bit shocky. I think they are depending on the speed of change, counting on it to give them swell new things they barely dreamed of before. Just last night at dinner my youngest told me that 1993 stuff is way out of fashion now. As I write this, it is January 4, 1994! (Not everything, he admitted, but lots of it.)

And as you create your own world view, and put together the things you need to take this path, you will discover that some of the stuff you learned as a youngster is still valid for you now, that some things no longer apply to the world you find yourself in, and that some things were invalid from the beginning.

In order for you to become an ethical being, you need to make these decisions and determinations yourself. No one else can do it for you. If you allow someone else to make your ethical decisions, you are giving away your own personal power, and you are not behaving ethically at all. You are behaving obediently. In my opinion, obedience is for children who do not yet have enough experience

under their belts to make cause and effect cor-
relations, and therefore can't be expected to
make wise ethical decisions. If you are not a
child, you should not be obedient. You are the
only person living your life, and therefore, you
are the only one qualified to make your life
decisions.

Yes, I know that means that you will have
to think a great deal.

I warned you about that in the introduction.

Get used to it.

It isn't like you have to start from a vacuum.

Begin with what you were taught as a kid.
Chances are that the rules and standards
drummed into you had a lot in common with
the basic law of the craft, although the reasons
for following them were different. You were
probably taught the golden rule, "Do unto others as you would have others do unto you."
Fine as far as it goes. Good for children. But I
think we can do better than that. We can "Do
unto others as they would have you do unto
them."

I told you in the beginning that this was
the hard path, not the easy one. And the farther along you go, the more your own ethics
will cause you to think, and then do things that
you know are right, even if you don't want to
do them.

I, for instance, consider myself an artist. I
am much more comfortable with images than

I am with these word things. Half the time, I
speak English like a second language. I never
wanted to write a book! But my ethics led me
to write this one, because I can not stand by
and see honest seekers looking and not finding
what they seek. I would consider it unethical
not to lend a hand.

So I have tried to share the tools that I
have discovered, Seeker, and I hope that they
will help you to build the ethical system that
fits you. It is my sincere desire that you will
realize that rules and reflexive reactions have
little place in a world that changes every
nanosecond; where every situation is unique,
and every individual you deal with is unlike
any other. In such a world, each case is a special case, and must be met with a special
answer. It is my goal to help you discover how
to reach those answers; honestly and non-
judgementally, with a heart filled with love,
understanding, wisdom and joy.

I want you to be able to steer your way
through your life, and find your heart's desire,
without harming anyone.

I hope that you realize that if you do harm
someone, you must make restitution. There is
no "forgiveness" on this path. Your "sins" are
not "wiped clean" with little or no effort on
your part. Here, "sins" are not part of the
question. Here we have only responsibility. You
are responsible for your own actions, and only
for your own actions. And if you break some-

thing with your actions, you are required to attempt to mend it with your actions, as well.

We all make mistakes, try as we might not to. The trick is to realize that we have, forgive ourselves, do our best to correct our mistake, and go on.

Sometimes, our ethics will cause us to change our entire lives. This takes great courage.

I have a friend who knew a Catholic priest. This priest was told something in confession that deeply troubled him. He felt that he could not simply assign a penance, and grant absolution for this thing. He had to tell the parishioner to come back in several days, by which time he would know what to do. The priest spent those days in serious soul-searching, and decided that no prayers he could assign would be great enough to cancel what the person had done, and he was not permitted to assign anything except prayers as penance. He told the man so in confession. The fellow went to a priest who didn't have such high ethical standards, and got his absolution. The priest left the Catholic church.

Do you understand, dear friend?

When you become ethical, when you begin to see the cause of your actions, when you truly take responsibility for everything you do, the easy way ceases to serve. It no longer works to say "Mea culpa" and be absolved,

because deep inside you know perfectly well that is not enough.

When you look within, and can find the answers there, you are beginning to arrive.

When you can shine the bright light of honesty on the dusty corners of your soul, and like what you see, you are well on your way.

When everything you look at, you look at with love and honesty, with a judgement unclouded by any sort of fear or prejudice, and you can decide clearly and wisely what you should do in each situation as it arises, you are there.

I, personally, am not there yet.

But I'm working on it!

The thinking and reasoning become easier all the time.

My prejudices are fading.

But in order for your prejudices to fade, you first have to know what they are. Mine were against stupidity, arrogance, selfishness, and greed. I tended to think that folk whom I perceived as having those character traits deserved whatever they got. I tended not to look farther back, and try to determine why they had those traits in the first place. I tended not to look ahead, and see if they were improving or getting worse. I tended not to look at them at all, in fact. I just saw a stupid person, and they instantly dropped below my mental horizon, so I didn't have to deal with them any more.

The quote at the beginning of this chapter is from *The Princess and Curdie* by George MacDonald. There are many gems of truth there, and I would like to share another with you. In the story, the old Princess, who is ancient but strong with her years, and has a great deal of power and wisdom about her, is sending the young miner Curdie to the King's court, to deal with the traitors and evil men which infest it. To this end, she has put Curdie through a painful ordeal (which she also feels, by the way) that will enable him to tell a good, honest man from one who is more animal than man by touching his hand. She explains that this is because all men, if they don't take care, go downhill to the animal's country. Knowing some of the miners, Curdie is not surprised.

"Ah!" [said the Princess] "But you must beware, Curdie, how you say of this man or that man that he is travelling beastward. There are not nearly so many going that way as at first sight you might think. When you met your father on the hill tonight, you stood and spoke together on the same spot; and although one of you was going up and the other coming down, at a little distance no one could have told which was bound in the one direction and which in the other. Just so two people may be at the same spot in manners and behavior, and yet one may be getting better and the other worse, which is just the greatest of all

differences that could possibly exist between
them."

This is why the prejudices must go. If you
encounter someone who is selfish, there is no
way to tell if they are more selfish or less selfish than they were a year ago. If they are less
selfish; if they are becoming more aware of the
reality of those around them, and thinking
more of others as being as important as themselves, I want to encourage them with everything that I have. I know that a large change
cannot occur all at once, that long accepted
patterns of behavior take time to change, and
that there will be periods of "backsliding" and
times when old habits take over. If the person
is sincerely trying to improve, though, they
need help and extra slack, not abrupt dis-
missal. So it is unethical to refuse them help
because of their behavior patterns until I know
for sure that they are headed downhill, not up.

We are not required to carry those who
have no intention of becoming ethical themselves forever.

But we are required not to be prejudiced,
not to pre-judge, those whose ethical decisions
we don't approve of.

If their decisions harm none, then we have
no right to make any kind of value judgement
here at all.

But even if their decisions do cause harm,
we have no right to dismiss them out of hand.
It is better, I think, to err on the side of helping

too much than on the side of not helping enough.

So examine your prejudices. (I have a friend who says that she keeps hers on a mental roll-a-dex, so that when she encounters a situation that she feels may be triggering one she can look to see.)

Cast the bright light of honesty on them until they dissipate like fog in the sun.

Keep working, and thinking, and trying to be better; and I assure you that you will be.

Let your appetites and habits rule you, have a pat answer for everything, and your ethics will slip away until you have none left.

Having ethics is like driving a car. Remember when you first learned to drive? You had to think about all of the mechanics of it, all the time. Hands go here, feet go there. Oh no! I'm turning the wheel too far! Ack! That's too far in the other direction! Where is that brake pedal? I know it has to be here somewhere!

Then, gradually, you learned how to do it, and it became easier. The traffic was constantly changing, but the mechanics were no longer such a problem. More simple things became almost reflexive, and less and less concentration was needed. Eventually, you got to the point where you could drive and hold a conversation, as long as the traffic wasn't too bad. (Although certain topics of conversation may still make you miss your turn!)

By now, you can probably drive without much trouble. You may even have an "autopilot" that will take you straight to work without any conscious effort on your part at all.

But if you don't keep at least some of your mind on the road, you will wind up in a pileup.

In just the same way, using your mind instead of a set of rules is hard at first. Every question is completely different than anything you have had to think through before. Correlating the cause and effect, and thinking through the ripples may seem almost paralyzing at first. Correcting for an error may result in an over correction that harms someone else. You may need to find the brakes, and use the old rules for a little while to get your breath back. (If so, go ahead. Most of the ones that don't judge other people are not bad, as far as they go. I just think they don't go very far.)

As you become more familiar with ethical living, you will find that certain questions follow certain patterns, and that you have thought a lot of this out before. Some things will become reflexive. You don't have to consider whether to use magic to cause someone to fall in love with you, for instance. You will just know that is wrong. The mechanics of having your brain with you at all times will be less and less of a problem. Eventually, you will be able to make rapid judgments for most things, and life will go pretty smoothly.

But don't make the mistake of letting your mind wander completely away, or you will end up in an ethical pileup.

Just as in driving, you may have only seconds to make the really important ethical decisions. Emergencies of all kinds are like that. And again as in driving, the more experience you have, the more likely you are to make a good decision in time.

Without the ability to drive, your freedom would be seriously curtailed. Without the ability to make good ethical choices, your freedom may need to be seriously curtailed.

So become a good ethical driver!

Go forth joyfully, with honesty and love and laughter and wisdom and all that good stuff. Steer carefully, enjoy your freedom, and write if you get work!

There is only one exercise for this chapter, but I want you to do it at least ten times.

Look in the paper, and find an ethical decision that needs to be made. Then make it, as if it was your decision to make.

Remember to use all the things you have learned in all the rest of this book. Honesty, love for yourself and the other people involved, good help, harming none, and clear exercise of will. Write down not only your conclusion, but the path you traveled to reach it. Be clear and non-

judgmental. You know what to do by now. You may want to choose a topic that is likely to come up in conversation, such as abortion or assisted suicide, so that you can discuss your ethics when it comes up. You may want to choose a topic you are likely to encounter in a more concrete way, such as the homeless, so that you can use your ethics when it comes up. Just remember, no matter what course of action you decide that you would follow, that each individual situation is a special case.

You may have noticed, during the course of this book, that I have made little distinction between "magical" and "mundane" ethics. This is because I don't think there should be a difference. Actions are actions, no matter what form they take. To carry the last analogy a bit further, you need to drive just as carefully in a Buick as you do in a Ford. The cars may be different, but the road and the destination are the same.

Go gladly into the world, and work consciously to make it a better place for all of us to live in!

BLESSED BE.

APPENDIX

This appendix is here for those who may have no idea what all this "Wicca" or "Craft" stuff is about, anyway.

I could, and will, point you toward a couple of excellent books. But just in case you have access to no book except this one, I feel that I should give you a bit of an explanation.

The following material is part of the introduction to the Book of Shadows that I hand out to all my students. Some of this I wrote myself. Some I put together from things that I was given to copy in my "own hand of write." The sources for those things were anonymous when I was given them 15 years ago. If I have stepped on anyone's toes in presenting it here, I do apologize.

In my tradition of the Craft, we study all of this stuff for a year and a day (at least) before initiation. This is because I strongly feel that initiation is not something to be entered into lightly. After all, once you are on this path, you will be drawn back to it forever, no matter how many lifetimes you may live. As they say, "Once a Witch, always a Witch."

Therefore, before I will initiate someone, I want them to be very sure just what they are getting into.

I am pretty nervous about letting you have this without me (or some other teacher) there to guide you. But at this point, I feel that it would cause more harm for you not to have it; and if you need a teacher, the Lady will provide you with one. That's Her job.

So here goes.

We are the Wicca; Witches; the secret children of the Goddess. We are a very ancient religion. Some say that our name means "wise ones". Others say it means "to bend". What it once meant is no longer important, for now it means both of those things, and many more besides.

In the dawn times, when mankind was young, we all worshiped the Mother, and Her consort, the Horned God of Fertility and the Hunt. We were simple people then, hunters and gatherers, and we lived in harmony with the earth.

But all things change, and we, too, changed. We learned to work with our Mother to bring forth the food we needed when and where we needed it - we invented agriculture. And we began to live in cities, and to make war with each other.

Gradually, we drew apart from our Mother, and as the long ages passed we forgot our first love, and the nurturing we had received. But some few still clung to the old ways, and learned the old skills. These were called Priestesses, or Witches, or Wise Ones; and they were feared, for their knowledge and their power.

When the new gods came into the land, and won the loyalty of the people by force and deceit, or by true acts of gentleness and loving kindness (for a good man may be found any-where - and every religion contains some truth) then the Gods of the old religion became the Saints and the Devils of the new.

For many years we lived together in har-mony. But at last greedy men seized control of the new religion, for the structure lent itself to controlling, and then the burning times began.

During those times, great change was upon the land, and a new light of reason dawned, and many in the ruling classes lost their power. But because there was great upheaval, the times were also troubled and uncertain; and all who were handy targets - the poor, women, and people whose color or philosophy did not coincide with the new ruling classes - were used to vent the anger and uncertainty of all the world.

Many were tortured, and countless thou-sands were killed - and we of the old religion hid for our lives; and were heard of no more, until people thought we were myth; a tale to frighten naughty children.

Then the laws against us were repealed -
for why outlaw a fairy tale? And in a new cli-
mate of tolerance, some are stepping forth
again; to separate the facts from the fiction,
and explain to all the world that we are simple
people; who desire nothing more than to grow
and learn in peace, to honor our Mother, the
Earth, and to worship the Gods we cherish in
the fashion we choose.

We are a polytheistic religion; we worship
the Mother, whom we call the Lady, and her
Consort, the Lord, as we have since the dawn
of time. There are many aspects of the Lord
and Lady, and we celebrate Their rituals using
many names.

Our circles are rich with chants and leg-
ends. Many are as old as the rocky hills. Many
are as new as the spring rain. For just as the
world grows and changes, with cycles repeating themselves year by year, so our religion
grows and changes, and yet the patterns and
rhythms repeat themselves again and again.

We do not perform sacrifices on Her altar,
for she does not delight in the shedding of
blood, but in joy and living. All acts of beauty
and love are sacred to Her, and we rejoice in
the celebration of life.

We are reverent, but seldom solemn. We
glory in laughter, and enjoy our worship.

There are three degrees of initiation in our
tradition of the craft. After studying for a year
and a day, and learning the basics of the craft,

a Pagan may ask for initiation. An Initiate of the first degree should study for an additional year and a day, gaining proficiency with the rituals and personal magic, at which time she may ask for elevation to the second degree. After another year and a day spent learning to see the patterns of the world and how to work within them, she may apply for elevation to the third degree. Witches of the third degree learn to step outside the patterns of this world, and mold them. Much of their time is spent teaching and counseling. (Folk will seek them out, whether they advertise or not. We joke that we walk around with "Priestess" or "Priest" stamped on our foreheads.)

We are a religion of Priestesses and Priests, and all Initiates are Priest or Priestess. As such, any Initiate may cast a circle for herself, or for a partner, for work or for prayer, or for a Pagan group, to teach and instruct them, and lead them in worship. Only remember to speak carefully to members of Pagan groups, and never forget that they are not Initiates.

If a Pagan wishes to become an Initiate, the first degree Witch should seek the advice and help of a second or third degree.

It is best to worship within a group, but this is not always possible.

Groups ideally consist of thirteen people; six couples and the High Priestess. She represents the Goddess, and leads the rites, assisted

by the High Priest she chooses. All should be in accord, with no dissension.

Attire varies from group to group. Many work sky-clad; that is nude. But when robes are worn, they are generally free-flowing and hooded. Each robe is the personal property of its owner, and traditionally it is never to be worn by any other person, nor is it to leave the possession of its owner. When it can no longer be worn, it is cremated.

However, in our tradition any covener may wear anything that "feels right". Circles have been celebrated in jeans and t-shirts! For the clothing, though it can serve to put one in the right frame of mind and tell the Twilight Self what is going on, is unimportant when that state of mind can be achieved at will.

Blessed Be!

Glossary

With any luck, most of the terms that I have used in this book have been explained in the footnotes or the appendix. But just in case you want to look stuff up more easily, here it is.

Athame: (A-tha-may) The sacred black handled knife of the Wiccae. This is traditionally a double-edged knife with a leaf shaped blade. Often Athames have sacred symbols on their hilts. They are not used for actual cutting, which is reserved for the Kerfan, or white handled knife, but for rituals.

Circle: A gathering of Witches or Pagans. We meet in Circles to worship and work magic. Sometimes the entire group is also known as the Circle. This can get a little confusing, "Our Circle is having a Circle where we will circle in a circle." You mostly have to figure it out from the context.

Craft: Short for "Witchcraft," or "the Craft of the Wise." Often used because it isn't as much of a buzzword as "Witch," which can cause instant and undesirable reactions in people who equate us with Satanists and think we eat babies.
    See *Wicca, Satanism*

Cult: In my definition, which is entirely mine, I think a cult is something that claims to be a religion, but spends 50% or more of it's entire resources (time, money, and energy) trying to convert other people. If you are spending as much time trying to convert others as you are worshipping whoever you worship, what is your actual point here?

Normally, Wiccan groups do not prose-lytize at all. We figure if you need us, you will find us. Therefore, by my definition, although we are occult, we are not a cult.

Esbat: Full Moon. Many groups meet for Circles during the full moon. These are called "Esbat Circles," so as not to confuse them with the Sabbat Circles held at the eight holidays.

See *Sabbat, Wheel of the Year*

God: See *Lord*

Goddess: See *Lady*

Grounding and Centering: The process of connecting oneself to the Earth (grounding) and aligning one's own energy flow (cen-tering). It is *absolutely necessary* to Ground and Center before one does any work at all involving energy or power. If you don't, you are likely to have a simply horrific headache, at the very least. You may also faint dead away, or become quite ill.

This is not the place where I can teach you this; and it's one of the areas where it

really helps to have a live teacher. There
are several books that can walk you
through it (Try *The Spiral Dance* by
Starhawk), and some tapes and so on. But
please, please, don't try doing Magic until
you have mastered this.

Initiate: Someone who has been through a
Ritual of Initiation, and taken certain vows.
(Mostly to protect the Craft and other prac-
titioners and dedicate oneself to the Gods.
They vary a bit from Group to Group.)

Although you can be self-initiated, I
think it's lots more fun to do it in a group.

The main point of the ritual, I believe,
is to open the doors of your far memory
(memories form previous lives) and remind
you of things you learned before. In my
case, and that of all but one of the people I
have initiated, this sparked far reaching
and overnight changes. These varied from
individual to individual; but no one was
quite the same afterward. (In the case of
the one, the changes seemed to happen
several weeks before the planned ritual
date. A sort of spontaneous initiation, if
you will. After all, as the saying goes, "The
Gods initiate. We just officiate.")

There is a great deal of controversy in
some circles about whether someone who
has not had an initiation ritual can call herself a Witch.

I, personally, think that there is already more than enough controversy in this world; and if someone calls herself a Witch, it's not my place to argue with her about her bona fides.

But I think that only someone who has experienced *some* form of initiation should call herself an Initiate. After all, that *is* what the word means.

See *Wicca, Witch*

Initiates Circle: A Circle for Initiates only. These may vary in form from non-initiates circles (often called Pagan Groves) or not. In my own tradition, magic is practiced only in the Initiates Circle, because a number of folk in our Grove cannot yet ground and center reliably, and would get terrific headaches from energy use.

See *Pagan Grove, Magic, Grounding and Centering*

Lady: The Goddess of the Wiccae. We also refer to Her by any of the names of any of Her aspects. She is a triple Goddess; Maiden, Mother, and Crone, and we identify ourselves with different aspects of Her at different points in our lives, as well as appealing to different aspects for different things. She is all encompassing, containing especially all creative and procreative properties, all aspects of nurturing and healing,

all forms of birth and rebirth, all growth and plenty. All women partake of Her nature, and are part of Her. All things are Her children. She is the earth, the moon, the stars and the rain. Together, the Lord and the Lady bring forth all the life that is on the earth.

Laughter: Something we do a lot of. We crack jokes, we commit faux paus, we knock over the altar candles and set ourselves on fire. (We are never hurt in any of this, mind you. We know how to extinguish ourselves quite well, thank you.) Not all groups do this to quite the extent ours does; but then, we all have our own traditions.

Lord: The God of the Wiccae. We also refer to Him by any of the names of any of His aspects. He is the Horned God of the Hunt, the Lord of Death and Resurrection. (The two are inextricably wed in our religion. You can't have one without automatically having the other.) We often refer to Him as the Laughing Lord. He is the Consort of the Lady, who dies and is reborn each year. He is sensuality, strength, music and lust. All men partake of His nature, and are part of Him. He is the sun, the sky and the wind. Together, the Lord and the Lady bring forth all the life that is on the earth.

Magic: Using knowledge and focused will to direct energy, and manifest a change in the world. This is stuff that must be done surely, carefully, and gently. If you don't know what you are doing, it can give you a killer headache. I'm not going to tell you how in this book, because I don't tell anyone how unless I know why they want to do this, and am sure that they can handle the energies involved.

If you want to learn this, please find a teacher whose ethics agree with yours. If you can't find a teacher, pray for one! Explain to the Lord and the Lady what you want, and why, and ask them to arrange things so you will meet your teacher, or someone who can introduce you to her.

Pagan: One who practices a religion that is not part of the Judeo-Christian-Islamic-Hindu-Muslim-Buddhist etc. bit. A Neo-Pagan usually is practicing a religion that harkens back to the old religions that were practiced before most of today's major religions came into being. These can take many forms, including the ancient African religions, Native American Shamanism, the old Greco-Roman stuff, the Celtic or Nordic traditions and so on. All Witches are Pagan. Not all Pagans are Witches, by any matter of means.

Pagan Grove: An outer circle, normally set up for teaching purposes, and led by a Wiccan High Priestess (HPS) and High Priest (HP.)

This is where folks start in many traditions (including mine) and learn what the Craft is about, and whether it is the right Path for them. This is the place you study for a year and a day before becoming an Initiate.

Groves tend to be fluid – but then, Pagan groups in general are like Lava Lamps. They flow, divide, join together, etc. with amazin' frequency.

Sometimes an entire grove of new students is started at once. Then people drop out as they lose interest, or become initiated, and a new Grove begins.

Sometimes, people join the Grove as they become interested, and then leave, decide to just stay Pagans, or become initiated, move on to the Initiate's Circles, and eventually hive off and start groups of their own.

I find the first easier to teach, because everyone tends to be more or less at the same place. But the second is more like a family because, in the words of one of my Coveners, "all the kids aren't the same age."

See *Initiate, Initiate's Circle*

Reincarnation: The belief that souls do not end at death, but wait for a time and then are reborn to live and learn on this earth again.

This is one of the central tenets of the Craft. Exactly how we do it is explained differently by different practitioners. (If you are studying Craft at all, you should know that we are a disorganized religion. In Simple Terms, that means that wherever you have five of us, you have seven religions.) But we all tend to agree that it is definitely something that we do, and many of us have the memories to prove it.

I tend to refer to this as "rolling up a new character." That undoubtedly comes from many years working for places like TSR, of Dungeons and Dragons fame. The Craft has absolutely nothing to do with D&D, which is just a game; but the simile is useful.

Sabbat: One of the eight holidays that Wiccans celebrate. A time for feasting, partying, and general merrymaking.

See *Wheel of the Year*

Satanism: The flip side of Christianity. These are folk who believe in the entire Christian mythos, especially the Catholic Christian mythos, and have decided to cast their lot with Evil instead of Good in the Great War that they think they are having.

Witches are not any form of Satanists. We can't be; we don't believe in Satan, and we don't promote evil. We have a saying, "In order to be a Satanist, you have to be a Christian. Otherwise, you are going to a great deal of trouble to insult a piece of bread."

Sky-Clad: Nude. Some traditions always practice sky-clad, on the principle that clothing interferes with the vibrations from the Earth. Since many of these same people practice indoors, and think that wood, steel and concrete don't interfere with these vibrations, I find myself wondering a bit. But if they feel that way, hey, they aren't hurting anyone.

Others practice sky-clad to show our freedom, which makes more sense to me, or to remember the burning times, when it is said that clothing identified the person and the person's social rank; so it was left outside the Circle for mutual safety. In those Circles, we are told, masks were also worn. With the parts usually seen covered, and the parts never seen uncovered, people were supposedly anonymous.

Some groups work sky-clad because it tends to be quite warm inside a Circle.

Some do, because they simply do. I think they need to examine this more closely.

In my tradition, we always do some things, like initiations, sky-clad; because it has long been done that way, and we are trying to rekindle old memories here. (According to *my* old memories, by the way, the purpose of being naked was to show that you were being born all over again. Your old life was over, and a new one starting. Babies are always naked when they are being born.) Other things, like Pagan Grove, and outdoor stuff in public places, are always done clothed, for obvious reasons. In other words, we take this, like everything else, on a case-by-case basis.

See *Initiation, Pagan Grove*

Wheel of the Year: The eight Sabbats in the Wiccan calendar. They occur at the Equinoxes and Solstices (the Quarters) and on the days marking the midpoints between them (the Cross-Quarters.) A short list of the names used by my tradition; **Yule** Winter Solstice; Candlemass or **Imbolc** Feb. 2; **Eostar** Spring Equinox; **Beltane** May 1; **Litha** Summer Solstice; **Lughnassad** August 2; **Mabon** Autumn Equinox; **Samhain** (pronounced *Sowen*) October 31.

Wicca: A neo-pagan religion which has it's roots in the ancient past, and it's revival in the late fifties and early sixties. The reason for much of the revival was that the law against Witchcraft, which carried capital punishment, was repealed in England in 1952. Yes. Nineteen. Less than fifty years ago. Therefore, some of the people who are responsible for the revival in this country are still alive today. They are amazingly interesting to talk to! For more information, read the Appendix.

Wiccae: Plural of Witch. One Witch, folk of the Wiccae, religion of Wicca, Craft, Witchcraft. Things Wiccan. All are terms for the neopagan religion of Wicca.
See *Wicca*

Witch: A practitioner of the Craft. (See *Craft*) A member of the Wiccae. (See *Wiccae*, and *Wicca*.) This term applies equally to either males or females.

Warlock, a term that the popular media applies to male witches, actually means "Traitor." A friend has suggested that it was used because male witches, by turning away from the Patriarchal religions, were seen as traitors to their sex.

G 12   WHEN, WHY … *IF*

Notes:

THIS is by no means an exhaustive list of books that you must read. Instead, it is a *very* short list of a handful of books that helped me the most when I was beginning to learn about the Craft, and a few books that I still find myself referring back to regularly. They are listed in alphabetical order by author.

There are tons of excellent books out there, and more are being published every day. This should help you get started if you don't know where to begin. Most of these books have lists of other books in them. I am including the ISBN numbers so that you can order them from your local bookstore if they don't carry them.

You may want to spend some time hanging out around your local new-age/occult/alternative bookstore, by the way, if you are lucky enough to have one in your area. It is often a good place to meet like-minded folk, have interesting discussions, and learn tons of new stuff. Just be warned that although many of these stores are wonderful, magical places, some are most definitely not. Go with your instincts here. If a place gives you the creeping heebie-jeebies (that's another technical term) don't tell yourself that you are simply making things up, and it must really be alright. If you feel like running away, Run Away! Not everyone is as ethical as you are striving to be.

The same holds true for the books themselves. Some of the things you will find in them will make instant sense, and feel like coming home. Some will be thought-provoking. Some you will find are not books to be set aside lightly – they are books to be hurled with emphatic force! (Not *these* books, I hope; but I have read some stuff in books that I found very unethical.) Always feel free to disagree with anything, to agree with anything, or to change and improve anything. That is how we synthesize new stuff. Growth is a continual process of change. Simply buying a package deal is not growth, it's just repetition and stagnation.

So find books, and enjoy them or disagree with them, as you will. Just remember to keep your mind with you at all times.

Adler, Margot. **Drawing Down the Moon**. Beacon Press 1979 ISBN 0-8070-3237-9.

This book is virtually required reading in most groups, and will explain stuff about the modern Neo-Pagan and Wiccan movement.

Broch, Janice and MacLer, Veronica. **Seasonal Dance**. Samuel Weiser, Inc. 1993 ISBN 0-87728-774-0.

A wonderful book with rituals, songs, and other fun stuff to celebrate the turning of the year.

Cunningham, Scott. **Wicca: A Guide for the Solitary Practitioner**. Llewellyn 1989 ISBN 0-87542-118-0 **Living Wicca**. Llewellyn 1993 ISBN 0-87542-184-9.

Anything by Scott is well worth reading. I particularly recommend these two, because they have more stuff in them about the actual religion of Wicca.

Slater, Herman (editor.) **A Book of Pagan Rituals**. Samuel Weiser, Inc. 1978 ISBN 0-87728-774-0.

Another book of rituals for all kinds of stuff.

Starhawk. **The Spiral Dance**. Harper & Row, 1979. ISBN 0-06-067535-7.

I consider this book to be Wicca 101. It is the only one I had in Okinawa, and is quite possibly the best introduction to the Craft ever written.

Valiente, Doreen. **An ABC of Witchcraft Past & Present**. Phoenix Publishing, Inc. 1973. Reprinted with corrections 1984. ISBN 0-919345-44-1.

If you want a glossary of terms Wiccan, this is the book for you. For some years, when I was beginning as a Solitary with no idea where to go for instruction, I used this book to help make sense of the other books!

H

My Favorite Books:

ROBIN WOOD is perhaps best known for her tarot deck, imaginatively called The Robin Wood Tarot, and for her many illustrations for Llewellyn Publications, including most of Scott Cunningham's books. She also works in the Fantasy Gaming genre.

She and her husband, Michael Short, spend a great deal of time traveling around the country to speak at Science Fiction conventions and Pagan gatherings. They are both third degree Witches in the Livingtree tradition, with 21 years of experience in the Craft between them. Put these things together, and you will find that this means that they do a great deal of counseling and training.

Robin wrote this book to answer some of the questions that she is asked a lot. She knows that she is far from perfect, but she is working on it!

If you need to, you can reach her at 3319 Greenfield Suite 102, Dearborn MI 48120. She is not very good at writing letters; so if you want a reply better include your phone number and give her permission to call collect.

The image of a boat on the cover of this book symbolizes the ethical structure you are building. A sound ethical boat has sail and rudder intact. It floats balanced between the air of knowledge and the waters of the emotions, steering its way among the sharp rocks of dilemmas that beset it.

The mist symbolizes our limited vision in even the best of circumstances. Limited; but clear enough if we watch carefully.

The knotwork on the sail shows the introspection necessary for sound ethical decisions; and once again balances the square of known facts with the circle of intuition.

The flag on the top of the mast shows bravery and vitality, because I think we should face life with courage.

And, finally, I named the book When, Why ...If because I figured you already had a pretty good idea of How and Where!

I hope you enjoy this book, and find it helpful (or at least thought provoking.)

Robin Wood

If you enjoyed this book, and are interested in Robin's work, please visit our website at:

http://www.robinwood.com

to see all the latest stuff. Thanks!